THE SINGING
HEART

Asian Poetry in Translation: Japan #20

Asian Poetry in Translation: Japan
Editor, Thomas Fitzsimmons

THE SINGING HEART

An anthology of Japanese poems
(1900-1960)
compiled and annotated by

Yamamoto Kenkichi

Translated by

William I. Elliott
and
Nishihara Katsumasa

Katydid Books
From University of Hawai'i Press

Katydid Books

#1 Balsa Rd., Santa Fe, New Mexico 87505

Web: katydid.com   Email: thomfitz@yahoo.com

First original Japanese edition published by Bungei Shunju Ltd., Japan.1981
as *Kokoro no Uta:* copyright © 2001 by Shizue ISHIBASHI & Yasumi ISHIBASHI.
The Singing Heart Copyright © 2001 by Katydid Books.
Translation Copyright © 2001 by William I. Elliott and Nishihara Katsumasa.
Cover art and design Copyright © 2001 by Karen Hargreaves-Fitzsimmons.

English Language translation rights reserved by Katydid Books license granted by
Shizue & Yasumi ISHIBASHI arranged with Bungei Shunju Ltd., Japan.

Distributed by University of Hawai'i Press
2840 Kolowalu St., Honolulu, HI 96822 FAX: (800) 650 7811
Web: uhpress.hawaii.edu   Email: uhpbooks@hawaii.edu

Produced by KT DID Productions.
Printed and bound in the United States of America on acid-free paper.

First Edition

CIP:
Library of Congress Cataloging-in-Publication Data

Kokoro no uta. English.
    The singing heart : an anthology of Japanese poems (1900-1960) compiled
and annotated by Yamamoto Kenkichi.
        p.cm.
    Includes index.
    ISBN 0-942668-59-6
    1. Japanese poetry--20th century .I. Yamamoto, Kenkichi, pseud.
II. Elliott, William I., III. Nishihara, Katsumasa. IV. Title.

PL782.E3 K5413 2001
895.6' 14408--dc21

                                                        2001050253

CONTENTS

Introduction
— 1 —

I
The World of Love
— 3 —

II
Death and Life
— 52 —

III
Human Existence
— 83 —

IV
Songs of Daily Life
— 91 —

V
Society and Human Beings
— 106 —

VI
Nature
— 127 —

VII
The Soul of a Traveller
— 142 —

VIII
Hometown Memories
— 175 —

INDEX
— 199 —

Introduction

Since the publication of *An Anthology of New Style Poetry* in 1882, eighty-five years of the history of the new poetry have passed [Trans.' note: *The Singing Heart* was published in 1967]. In that period so many kinds of poets and poetic experiments have appeared that we have been astonished at the evidently unending series of changes that Japanese poetry has undergone and continues to undergo. I wonder whether people are willing to apply the term "poetry" to the variety of avant garde poems being written today as well as to the poems in the early anthology.

In 1904 in *The Poetry of Tōson*, Shimazaki stated that "The time of the new poetry has come at last" and in 1909, in a prefatory remark to his *Heretics*, Kitahara Hakushū stated that "The life of poetry lies in suggestion rather than in an explanation of things." Then in 1917 in a preface to his *Howling at the Moon*, Hagiwara Sakutarō stated that "Poetry is simply a melancholic solace for sick souls and the lonely" and Nishiwaki Junzaburō, in his 1926 essay on poetry—"Profanus"—wrote that "Poetry is a means of calling attention to this banal reality by means of a certain unique interest, perhaps a mysterious sense of exultation." Since these various words were written, much has happened. Just what poetry is can only be asked again and again in every succeeding period, for as long as human beings live. Definitions—answers—are innumerable and so we shouldn't be surprised at the kaleidoscopic changes that have occurred in the last eighty-five years.

The poems selected here aren't much more than a handful thrust into the rapid stream of Japanese poetry. I believe, however, that even among these few poems there are interesting experimental poems, the lives of poets reflected therein. I have chosen mainly up-to-date colloquial poems, some old-fashioned fixed verse forms, namely new style poems, and then a smaller number of traditional tanka and haiku. When we speak of Japanese poetry we cannot completely neglect tanka and haiku, at least in my personal view.

In the beginning this book was to be one of a series called *Books of Life*. This is why I categorized the poems under the rubrics Love, Death, Life, Living, Society, Nature, Traveling and Hometowns. Writers whose poems did not fit under these rubrics I had, unfortunately, to omit. This was perhaps unavoidable. Avant garde poets in particular appear to be indifferent to themes or meanings; from the outset they reject the classification "poetry". I feel it a pity that I could not net this sort of poem, but spilt milk is spilt and there's an end to it.

What I'm indicating here is how chaotically swirling the actual world of Japanese poetry is. I hope that out of this wonderful morass readers will pluck their favorites. It is said that poetry nowadays is in vogue and though many books of poems and poetry criticism have appeared it is doubtful that any clear formal direction for poetry can emerge out of the chaos.

In the East poetry from early on was written for the speaking of one's own heart and mind, and this idea jibes with *The Singing Heart* as the title of this book. Poets today, however, do not accept that as the function of poetry, for as I said before poetry must constantly be redefined. Ancient philosophers always assumed that ideas, like history, will go on changing and yet they also assumed that word and will must match in the process of historical change. I should like readers to consider this book's title in that context. This collection of poems reflects some Japanese hopes and ambitions in the three eras of Meiji, Taishō and Shōwa.

I

The World of Love

Shimazaki Tōson's first book of poems —*Young Herbs* —was the first outcry of the romantic sentiment in the adolescent period of modern Japanese poetry. One way to capture the hearts of young readers is to cry out with a bold, fresh, loving heart.

Kitamura Tōkoku, regarded by Tōson as his superior, stated that "Love is the secret medicine in life. Life is finally lived when love is born. What is the taste of life without love?" In the 1890's this was indeed a challenging manifesto and a shocking one to Tōson and his contemporaries.

Such young writers as Kitamura, Tōson, Baba Kochō, Togawa Shūgetsu, Hirata Tokuboku and Hoshino Tenchi in a magazine they published called *Bungakukai* (The Literary World) raised the banner of the new romanticism in Japan. Self-consciously and seriously devoted to the pursuit of true, sincere literature, they competed with one another in love affairs involving the new sort of young high- school girls. Confucian morality dictated that at the age of seven boys and girls should no longer share the same classroom. For the first time, in the 1890's, boys and girls were, inspired by a gradually changing mentality, to have the opportunity of free association and friendship.

Tōson was baptized a Christian at the age of seventeen in 1888 and went on to Meiji School which was founded by Christian missionaries. There he boarded in Hepburn House, constructed after Western architectural ideas. Invited to attend a literary society meeting, he met many female students and listened raptly to their English recitation and songs. He frequently participated in co-educational gatherings and visited the home of a Presbyterian missionary. Through the influence of a beautiful widow of the titled class, he was introduced to the world of politics. He had imagined that he might one day enter government service and found parallels between himself and the young impoverished Disraeli.

His reading at the time included Shakespeare, Goethe and Byron, all of them possessed of a romantic element like a sweet, murmuring tickle. Their stories of young love were radically different from the stories of love involving prostitutes in the writings of Chikamatsu and Saikaku. Tōson and other contemporary writers tried to live out the tales they read in Western literature. Tōson became a teacher at Meiji Girls' High-School and fell passionately in love with a student of his called Satō Sukeko. This passion failed. Kitamura for his part fell in love with Ishizaka Miyako and married her. Another writer named Kunikida Doppo married Sasaki Nobuko but their marriage failed in short order. There was also an international marriage involving the novelist Mori Ōgai and a German dancer named Elise.

Tōson's adolescent novel *Spring* reveals how he and his fellow writers lived—in life and in literature—after the fashion of European Romantic poets. To live and to die for love was for them life's primary duty. Female virginity was thought to be of the first importance, as was the pure, naïve feeling accompanying first love.

Tanka and haiku as verse forms were not considered apt for the expression of such feelings; European forms of poetry were thought preferable and Tōson was the first singer in this new style.

The following poem was the most loved and cherished of all of his poems.

SHIMAZAKI TŌSON (1872-1947)

First Love
(from *Young Herbs*)

Her hair upswept,
she stood beneath an apple tree,
and as she came nearer he noticed
flowers held in her hair by a comb.

Gently extending her white hand,
she offered him an autumn apple
not yet quite ripe,
and he felt the first tremors of love.

As his breath brushed
the hair on her neck
he felt he was filling her heart, from his,
with the wine of first love.

To this tree in the orchard
footprints somehow had worn a gentle path.
He trembled when she asked,
'Who, I wonder, made this little path?'

Until a girl was fourteen or fifteen, a certain hair style was prescribed: upswept in both front and back, the back done into a kind of bun. By this style her age and innocence were at once known.

Tōson is here recalling a pastoral scene from his youth in the town of Magome. After the razing of a samurai's house; mulberry bushes were planted on the site and amid the mulberries stood a small apple orchard. A white stone wall separated his house from that of his first young love—called Obun—which was visible above the stone wall.

Although the poem is rooted in reality it is obviously highly idealized, which is a result of Tōson's effort to transfer the atmosphere of such European "romances" as *Romeo and Juliet* into a Japanese setting. But the apple orchard named above did not in fact exist in Magome. It was deliberately planted in the poem by Tōson. For the Japanese, the atmosphere of European love was exotically represented by grapes and apples. So, too, the Bible, which influenced Tōson, abounds with fruits. In the Song of Solomon, 2:3, one finds, "As an apple tree among the trees of the wood,/So is my beloved among the young men."

The poem's third stanza is beyond the experience of teenagers in Tōson's 19th C., recognizing which the poet at first deleted it; however, an awkwardness then characterized the poem's movement and so he restored it. In Chinese poetry one form calls for an introduction, development, a turning and a conclusion, and Tōson had left the pattern unfortunately broken, whence he restored stanza three.

Nige-Mizu
(from *Young Herbs*)

As twilight settles on the grass
I pause and, so it seems,
am overcome a while and pass
into a world of dreams.

And soon the tears begin to flow.
I stand around the flowers;
a lover, you alone can know
the secret that is ours.

I think of how our love has fared.
Our love is sinful, yes.

And yet the dangers that we dared
were lovely, nonetheless.

It comes to this: by work and prayer,
by prayer and work to win
release from guilt and worldly care;
forgiveness for my sin.

And one day, hand in hand at last,
we'll gladly walk ahead,
however threatening the mist,
however dark the dread.

The poem given above is a parody of a hymn whose words were written by Phoebe H. Brown in 1825. The Japanese translation was done by Uemura Masahisa, whereas another more recent translation also exists and thus the original lyrics have been modified. Uemura was one of the founders of Meiji Gakuin University, founded by American Presbyterian missionaries, and from that school the poet Tōson graduated. He himself in university chapel services doubtless sang Brown's words. The hymnal stanza in English (Brown's poem is an example) consists of alternating eight-and six-syllable lines. The Japanese preference is for alternating lines of seven and five syllables, a pattern that creates for them a fresh, clean feeling. Here is Brown's hymnal lyric:

I Love To Steal Awhile Away

I love to steal awhile away,
From every cumb'ring care,
And spend the hours of setting day
In humble, grateful prayer.

I love in solitude to shed
The penitential tear
And all his promises to plead
Where none but God can hear.

I love to think on mercies past,
And future good implore;

And all my care and sorrows cast
On him whom I adore.

I love my faith to take a view
Of brighter scenes in Heav'n;
The prospect doth my strength re-new,
While here by tem-pests driven.

Thus, when life's toilsome day is o'er,
May its departing ray
Be calm as this impressive hour,
And lead to endless day.
         A-men

This pious prayer Tōson changed into a passionate love song. For him Christianity was not so much a system of belief as it was a door opening into the new current of exotic Western thought. In changing a hymn into a quasi-erotic love-song he had already abandoned Christianity and had decided not to attend services again, thinking himself a hopeless sinner bound for the darkness of the after-life.

What did this experience mean to him? The poem lacks the innocence of "First Love" and indeed borders on licentious love where love is more often than not thought to be sin, or, using the title of a Tōson novel, *Transgression.* In another novel—*New Life* —incest is explored. I don't want here to ask whether at the time he had such a romantic relationship that he cared not a whit about hell or other consequences, for we should not, as readers of poetry, confuse poetry and autobiography.

Tōson's intention is clear in parodying the hymn: that regardless of any consequences he dared to declare for romance as over against faith. The Japanese title of the poem is "Nige-Mizu," (lit., "escaping", or" moving water"). This refers to an ancient phenomenon associated with the Musashino Plain (now a district of Tokyo). It was the common visual hallucination everyone who has driven across the desert is familiar with. An old waka reminds us that however often the water appears, it escapes, and vice versa. It is in the world but not of the world. The poem title, then, refers to a real but fleeting—an unattainable—love.

MIKI ROFŪ (1889-1964)

After a Kiss
(from *Deserted Garden*)

'Didn't sleep well?'
'No.'

Flowers blooming
Mid-day
In May.

A grassy bank
In sunlight.

'Eyes closed, I'm dead,'
You answered.

This is one of Miki's most beloved poems. Young lovers lying on the grass, whispering, the sun warm and the grass lovely—Miki condenses this scene into a few words. To the question, "Are you sleepy?" she answers that she is not and that she'd like to die just as she is, eyes closed in recollection and contentment. The poem is quite transparent in conveying the scene and the lovers' feelings. The poem's title recalls the simplicity of waka or haiku. The subject measures a moment of ecstasy that readers will quickly feel. At a later point in his career, however, Miki moved on to become a symbolist in poetry.

Hometown

The trees of Ono,
my hometown....
A flute reverberated in boughs
that also trembled beneath the moon.

The girl beside me,
impassioned,
listened to the flute
and wept.

Even after ten years
does your heart remain as ever?
Even though you are a mother,
do your tears still flow?

This poem, from Miki's collection *Deserted Garden*, was written when he was eighteen, though it recalls an experience of his when he would have been eight. Of course, the event is purely imaginary. The pastoral scene is surely banal, as is the notion of a young girl weeping at the sounds of the flute. It is only in the third stanza that the poem comes alive, passing quietly over a decade to the girl's present status as wife and mother. The incidents of that decade are an indifferent blank. At any rate, he now asks her whether her heart remains as passionate as ever, recalling that boy. Thus stanza three enlivens a poem that would otherwise be flat. Stanza three, then, combines two aspects of the four-fold Chinese poetic principle: after the introduction and development come the turning and conclusion.

KITAHARA HAKUSHŪ (1885-1942)

Unrequited Love
(from *Tokyo Seasonal Poems*)

Red and gold fall from the acacia
in autumn twilight, falling, falling....
in my flannel gown, unrequited love,
fishermen pulling their boat ashore....
falling, falling, your soft breath falling,
red and gold fall from the acacia.

This reads like a folk-song. The famed novelist Nagai Kafū was particularly fond of the repeated "falling, falling," which was a phrase often used by ordinary people in the Kansai dialect (especially in Osaka). That atmosphere is aroused by the phrase. But in fact the setting of the poem is probably Tokyo. The tree was the black locust, sometimes called "false acacia," and around 1910, when this poem was written, the false acacia was a rare tree in Japan. Even now, however, in 1967, certain streets lined with these trees can be found.

The reference in 1.4 to a boat being towed ashore has two meanings: the second meaning is that of the name of a street. There was in Sumida Ward in Tokyo a street called Boat-Towing Street running along the west bank of Boat-Towing River. Such young poets as Kitahara, Kinoshita Mokutarō and Yoshii Isamu were in their youth filled with a nostalgic longing for the open, friendly atmosphere that prevailed along Boat-Towing Street in that district of eastern Tokyo (adjacent to Tokyo Bay).

Children have long since stopped wearing such expensive flannel gowns, yet in those days it was a special pleasure to have that soft fabric next to one's skin. There is a rather harsh juxtaposition in the poem, pitting one-sided love against the softness of the flannel. The feeling juxtaposes distress and sweetness.

The crowning achievement of the poem is made possible by the repetition found in the first and last lines. The image is deliberately unclarified in that facial features, for instance, cannot be precisely distinguished in the twilight that immediately precedes darkness. Kitahara manages to achieve the same effect as that achieved by the tanka and haiku poets of the time in the interplay of light and colors.

While the poem does not in itself directly speak of unrequited love, the theme of such in older literature frequently draws upon the abalone, which resembles a bivalve but is in fact a univalve and has therefore become a symbol of one-sided love. Futabatei Shimei had translated Turgenev's novel *First Love*, which is in fact a story of one-sided love even though the title evokes in us the sense of a new, a fresh, love. In general, unrequited love is of course seriously distressing; in this poem, however, a semi-sweet or soft element is operative. The poet aims at a faint, indistinct sort of unrequited love. He seems to take pleasure in such love; to be amused by it.

"White Balcony"
(from *Paulownia Flowers*)

Longing,
I stand in the precincts
of the monastery
and hear the bell
close out the day.

Lying alone,
I feel, without you,
dead.

In the darkness
cherry blossoms are stark, stark white.

Recalling the herbal blossom,
pierced by its sharp scent,
I gaze
at your white face
that dances before me.

At dusk
I stand
on a white balcony,
wondering
where you are.

I see you
on your white balcony.
On this lucky night
I wonder:
is the bachelor's button blooming there?

(from "Sorrow")

Smoke rising
from the incense
split into wisps
of purple and white.
I wept.

In the last moments
before we parted
forever,
the dahlia was red—
dazzlingly red.

You stared
at the red peony
and, weeping,

said
you wanted my child.

I was starkly
aware of you
slumped over
in the black carriage,
distraught with tears.

Overcome,
and weeping,
we saw
red clover blooming
in the prison yard.

Just before
you entered the prison
I saw you tilt the hat
that hid your face
to gaze at a red flower.

Released from prison,
I was so startled by
the whiteness of your toes
that suddenly
I embraced you.

In May
the red poppy
was so gorgeous
that I felt I could stab us both
and have us die together.

In 1910 Kitahara moved to Harajuku in Tokyo. A woman called Matsushita Toshiko lived next door—the woman along with whom he would later be imprisoned. In his writings he tells us that she had been abandoned by her husband on account of his having acquired a mistress. To Toshiko, of course, this was an insupportable insult and Kitahara, aware of this, wanted to support her, in ultimate consequence of which he himself was ruined. In those days, divorce was disallowed and adultery, so-called, was a criminal offense. In the tanka collected as "White Balcony" the career of Kitahara and Toshiko's forbidden love is traced; whereas "Sorrow" treats the prison episode which so profoundly affected him that he constantly thought of suicide; however, he recovered and achieved satori, that ecstatic enlightenment sought after by Buddhists. He wrote various collections of tanka based on his religious joy, among them *Glittering Mica*, *A Sparrow's Eggs* and *A Silver Top*.

Weather Beaten
(from *A Silver Top*)

Transformed, but still a mere man,
I wanted even more
to surrender to religious joy
and so expose myself to wind and rain.

Maimed on my journey
along the dark road of my sin,
my agony in that dark hell
seemed endless.

Kitahara and Toshiko married and moved into a house on the Miura Peninsula where they lived for one year. The world they lived in now, consisting of the sea, fish glittering in sunlight, women abalone divers, vegetables in the garden and the delight of local children at play, was a rapturous blessing that would appear in his ongoing tanka. Unfortunately, this happiness and their relationship collapsed after one year.

(from *Glittering Mica*)

Suddenly
I embraced you
in joy and contentment.
You laughed and closed your eyes—
you, my wife.

(from *A Sparrow's Eggs*)

I recall how your eyes,
so large and laughing,
grew cold.
We turned our backs to one another
and felt anger in our hearts.

However much
we suffered in prison
we were yet in love!
Now......
this suffering seems unbearable.

We shall divorce
and yet, man and wife,
we were in love.
Recalling our love,
I sink into despair.

The division is made
and yet some unseen bond
binds us and we weep.
Another day has passed
into evening.

The little girl
hidden beneath her hat
stooped and, hands behind her back,
looked
at the red touch-me-nots.

The child's hat in this tanka and the girl's posture recall Toshiko handcuffed and
hiding her face beneath her own broad-brimmed hat as she entered prison. In
the yard she, too, had stooped to peer at some red flowers. This is what
Kitahara recalled in the composing of this tanka.

YOSHII ISAMU (1886-1960)

(from *Songs in Praise of Sake*)

My heart smiles
because
drinking
has made me several friends
and many acquaintances.

I listen
to the bitter wind
and somehow
understand why you left me.
The feeling in your heart.......

I gasp at the thinness
of your body—so thin
your obi is absurdly long
when you drop it on the sand.
Has love wasted you, I wonder?

Lake Biwa is so lovely
it draws crowds
of even lovelier girls—
who avoid me
on your account.

Waves
have washed away
your name in the sand.
Who was he, I wonder? And who
will wash away your name from my heart?

I stand on the beach and see
at dusk the flickering of fires
on my beloved Izu hills,
and see down deeply
your dancing figure.

These things deeply move me:
the roar of the distant sea,
the cry of the gulls
and
your tenderness.

(from *Songs from Gion*)

Gion is so dear to me.
At rest, I hear
beneath my lacquer pillow
the trickling of a creek,
suspiciously like tears.

I listen sympathetically
to the stories told me
by the maid Oasa
in the geisha house—
past love so similar to mine.

My feelings perhaps
so much like his own,
I forgot to say greetings
to the traveller who stands gazing
at the surface of the Kamo River.

The dancing girl Kichiya,
just recovered from her illness,
stands on the river bank
staring at the spreading mugwort.
How pitiable she seems.

Walking along the bank,
feeling bereft,
I trod on the wort,
and the scent that rises
reminds me of you.

The really finest feeling
I ever have,
the dancing girl says,
is the moment in which
my long obi begins to swirl.

In the dead stillness of night
the bell in the temple
where the cork tree grows
sounds and resounds, falling like snow,
and I cannot sleep.

Such young poets of the New Poetry School (such as those belonging to the School of the Morning Star), namely, Kitahara Hakushū, Kinoshita Mokutarō and Yoshii Isamu, broke off into a group of their own, based on estheticism, called the " Pan Club." All of these young poets were idealists and all of them except Yoshii eventually modified their stance. Yoshii alone remained loyal in his life, as in his writing, to estheticism. Unable to live a life of merely moderate decadence, he abandoned his home and utterly surrendered to a life of unmitigated decadence to the very end of his days.

The tanka that I have selected from *Songs in Praise of Sake* and *Songs from Gion* clearly suggest the life of the libertine.

In the former collection we learn of a girl he met one summer while staying in a temple in Kamakura. The tanka in that collection are not psychologically convoluted but they accurately capture the breath of a young man in love. The love is not impassioned; one hears in it, instead, a sigh of ennui.

The mood of the latter collections is, likewise, one of fatigue. Not a man to commit himself to one love, he immersed himself in an unrelieved epicureanism, celebrating wine, women and song, while distancing himself from "society". The girls Oasa and Kichiya perfectly evoke the sentiment of Yoshii's world.

WAKAYAMA BOKUSUI (1885-1928)

(from *The Voice of the Sea*)

There is something sad
about that white bird

for it belongs
neither to the blue sky
nor to the blue sea.

Can you imagine me,
a man in love,
engulfed
by the loneliness
of the sea?

Look at the mountain,
sunlit!
Look at the sea,
sunlit!
Ah, your lips....

At times
you are struck
speechless
by the sight
of the sea.

How would you respond
if you were courted,
wooed,
by
the great god of the sea?

When we kiss
we feel the kiss could last forever.
When the kiss has ended
I return to earth
and see your black hair.

On this autumn night
your face, so lightly made up,
exudes a loneliness
and all around us
is quietude.

We sit face to face
beside the paper lantern.
This night in spring
is utterly tranquil.
Do you, I wonder, feel like crying?

(from *Singing Alone*)

Now's the perfect time
to go and see
the mountain
we've never seen before.
Can you endure the solitude?

No one to rely on,
no place to go,
you, too,
like me,
are a wanderer.

Just ahead,
where our love will end,
a few
early summer flowers
will begin to bloom.

(from *Parting*)

The grasses of autumn
wither
and descend to the depth
of their sorrow.
This I dedicate to you.

[In the early spring of 1907 I went to the seaside with a certain woman by whose side, night and day, I continuously recited tanka.]

Children on the beach
linger around the boat.
Their father will soon
depart on a sad journey.
The sea gulls cry.

She is so lovely
these days
that I came here
to buy wine
to lift her spirits.

Our love
having just begun,
this tinge of sadness
makes me wonder
why I should be sad.

Like chestnuts
growing, strangely,
at the top of the tree,
so,
our lonely love.

The love tanka above I selected from his first three collections. The third one—
Parting—includes the first two collections, so it may well be said that the
original source of these tanka is the third one, *Parting*. In this tanka collection
the way Bokusui brings out his best lyrical power strongly impressed the young
of that day.

Bokusui, nearing twenty-four, went to the beach called Nemoto in Awa,
Chiba Prefecture, in company with a woman. At first he didn't seem to know
that she had already experienced marriage and was older than he.

He was at the time opposed to the manner of "The Morning Star" school,
typically represented by Yosano Akiko's technical, artificial, fanciful manner
of tanka. To the contrary, he sought to sing a full-throated song of tanka with
verisimilitude of genuine feelings and thought. He was in a way a born lyric
poet. It is almost impossible to find such a passionately lyrical tanka poet
among modern Japanese poets. In spite of the brilliant colors of the sea and
mountains and the glittering sunlight of Awa in the southern country, there is

an air of melancholy even in his love-sick, flaming heart. It is the mood of melancholic love that runs through these tanka.

Compared to the style of "The Morning Star" group, Bokusui's tanka is shot through with the rare, vivid and genuine sentiment of life itself.

Again, many of these tanka selected here were loved by all young people of those days.

ISHIKAWA TAKUBOKU (1886-1912)

"Unforgettable People," Part 2
(from *A Handful of Sand*)

The voice I heard in my dream
quite by chance
I heard for such a long time;
and yet now have not heard
for a long time. A pity.

Roaming the countryside,
A simple traveller,
I happened to meet
A girl
Of whom I asked directions.

What I said
with no particular intent
you heard
and heard
with no particular intent.

The picture of her
is with me still:
that black-eyed maiden
whose eyes absorbed
all the light in the world.

The important words
I wished to say to you

on that occasion
I failed to say,
and they still remain in my heart.

I cannot seem to feel
the reality of what I heard—
that you fell ill,
that you got well—
because we are so far apart.

I hope you can understand
how my heart danced
when I saw
on the street
a girl who looked like you.

To chase
the shadows
from my heart this morning
I would only need
to hear your voice.

If I said to you
I'd like to see you again
before I die,
I wonder,
would you nod in understanding?

In Hokkaido
in the Ishikari District
in the suburbs of Miyako
stands your house, and in the garden
apple blossoms probably litter the ground.

Have I,
in these three years,
in response to
your three long letters,
now written to you a fourth time?

In the preceding eleven tanka Ishikawa recalls various people met along the way in his travels in Hokkaido in 1907-08. "Unforgettable People" is divided into two parts. Part 2 treats exclusively the one woman Tachibana Chieko, a fellow teacher at Yayoi Elementary School in Hakodate where, on June 11, 1907, he was employed as a substitute teacher. His work there lasted a mere three months and during that time their relationship developed only as a friendship ("I happened to meet/a girl/of whom I asked directions."). In his diary he comments on his fellow workers. Of Tachibana he writes that she stood erect, like a dappled lily. She herself was completely uninterested in him on account of his tendency to be lazy. She had no way of knowing that he was an up-and-coming poet of the Morning Star group of poets. They spoke on only two occasions. April 1908 found him apart from his family, living alone in Tokyo and longing for Chieko, even though they had been nothing but acquaintances.

We can see him going through a familiar human process in life's journey in that at a considerable remove he now idealizes the woman and believes himself hopelessly in love. As in the first tanka, it is the remembered sound of her voice that facilitates the crystalization of his feelings.

In the correspondence volume of his collected works, only two of the letters that he wrote to her are given. One of the letters refers to her release from the hospital (the letter is dated June 2, 1908) and thus the sixth tanka above is based on fact. The other letter (dated December 24, 1909) states that he has sent her a copy of A Handful of Sand and adds words to this effect: "You will notice in twenty-some of these collected tanka that there is a wandering soul who wrote by way of consoling himself." He adds, "Please take pity on me." He uses tanka as a way of appealing to her heart.

Some time later she married into the Kitamura family, who were dairy farmers. As a token she sent Ishikawa a quantity of butter. They never met again.

(from *A Sad Toy*)

In Ishikari
in the Sorachi district
there is a meadow
and from there a bride
sent me some butter.

Burying my chin
deep inside my overcoat collar

I stopped on the street
late at night to listen
to a voice that sounded like hers.

The voice was of course Chieko's, now echoed in that of another woman. In the authorized biography Kindaichi Kyōsuke, Ishikawa's close friend, writes as follows: "Somewhere we once happened to hear a woman's beautiful voice coming from inside a house. [He] froze, as if thunder-struck. This astonished me. Again, when we were looking at lovers in a sidewalk stall along Hongō Street he seemed to hear a voice and all of a sudden blurted out, 'That's her voice exactly!' This, too, astonished me."

SAITŌ MOKICHI (1882-1953)

Ohiro
(from the first edition of *Red Radiance*)

When at night in my futon
I try to pass
into the depths of sleep,
the familiar warmth is gone
and I miss her familiar face.

Although our love was brief,
so short-lived,
our parting
broke my heart
and I writhe in agony.

I longingly recall her eyes,
nearly closed,
and she is gone again,
though not from my heart.
How many nights have passed......?

She went away in sadness.
Even the light at sundown
seems sad

as it plays on the wisteria
brushed by her shoulder.

A woman
with a fragile soul
came into my life
flowing in
and...away....

The very moment of daybreak:
the delicious
flicking of her black eyelashes
struck me then—
and now.

'Your fingers are so cold,'
she said,
and encouraged my embrace
while the night snow fell
silently.

Our lips touched
and yet the brown brick wall
around the madhouse
shone so violently vermilion,
we could not relax.

My life flares up
like the last flash of a candle flame
and your teasing whisper—
'No, don't...!'—
dies into silence in my embrace.

She is gone.
And in my loneliness
and passion
my heart glows like those fires
on the distant mountain.

'Poor girl...'—
a premonition.
As I brush her eyelashes
with my fingertip
I could nearly die.

I rub the inkstone
to prepare vermilion ink
and to prepare myself for work
and yet tonight, as always,
my mind goes out to her.

Inside the flower
that round shape
the light blue
of lapis lazuli
is my lover's eye.

Let your eyes
always be as lovely
as they are
when you stare at stars
that come into the eastern sky.

The "Ohiro" series of tanka and a series called "My Deceased Mother," both dealing with separation, come from the book *Red Radiance*. Love poems and elegies constitute two central themes of the first imperial anthology (756) called the *Man'yōshū* (10,000 Leaves Collection).

Many poets and critics have pondered about the actual identity of Ohiro, but she remains a mystery. In a book entitled *Four Decades of Writing Tanka*, Mokichi writes: "Is this woman an actual person, a poetic fiction, or what? There is no use trying to discover any actual identity. Nakamura Kenkichi, my friend, knew some of the relevant facts, but he is dead."

The Mokichi-Ohiro relation began at the end of 1912. By mid-April in 1913 he tried to end their relationship and felt remorse over this. Although we do not know who she was, the tanka in which these lines occur "...the brown brick wall/around the madhouse" shows two lovers embracing and looking at the vermilion sunrise reflected on the madhouse wall, which scene allows us to imagine, e.g., that she might have been a nurse. The hospital where he was employed was the Sugamo Mental Hospital, but we do not know whether Ohiro was associated with that one or the hospital operated by Mokichi's physician-father.

At any rate, the woman appears to have relocated in a distant city. In the "Ohiro" series he recites rueful songs reflecting his loneliness and songs, too, remembering their embraces. They are memories out of which he attempts to reconstruct actual events. "I longingly recall her eyes, nearly closed," relates to the line of a subsequent tanka: "...as I brush her eyelashes..." and to:

> 'No, don't...!'—
> dies into silence in my embrace.

He draws a very vivid picture of Ohiro by night. His recital of his own tanka was always highly sensual.

That Mokichi longed rather for a woman's body than her heart is something pointed out by many critics. This is certain. And yet we must suggest that Mokichi truly believed in the validity of a foreordained encounter, which added a dimension to the sexual union. He believed the moments after ecstasy to be unique and irrecoverable, and this is why after parting he directs rueful and loving feelings toward her body. His homage to the female body, therefore, approaches the metaphysical.

> A woman
> with a fragile soul...

is an expression borrowed from the work of his poetic master, Itō Sachio: "A lover/with a fragile soul..." "Fragile" here perhaps includes pure melancholy, but Mokichi's usage enables us to imagine a woman with fine skin and a melancholic disposition.

In early July of 1913 the tanka poet Shimaki Akahiko (1876-1926) asked Mokichi to travel with him briefly to Suwa. On the way he dropped by a certain town where stood the ruins of a castle (perhaps in Kōfu). There he met Ohiro. The following three tanka come from his collection "Stones on the Roof," included in *Red Radiance*:

> I have purposely come here,
> having crossed many mountains,
> to ask for the love of

a woman
with a fragile soul.

When we met and embraced
in the ruins of the castle
myriad seeds of the red balsam flower
lay thick at our feet,
everything washed in the setting sun.

The sky seemed to withdraw.
We embraced at sundown
and on the hill behind us
a small cave caught
and swallowed the soft light.

In this section only these three tanka refer to Ohiro. They are an epilogue to the "Ohiro" section, for she here makes her final appearance in the book.

TAKAMURA KŌTARŌ (1883-1956)

The Lost Mona Lisa
(from *Steps Along the Way*)

Mona Lisa walked away
leaving behind that mysterious smile
and the soft silvery words, 'Be a good man!',
faint, soft, sad words from far away;
like a wife of a victorious returning shogun,
casting an eye both warm and distant
and speaking quietly, softly,
her voice silvery.
Mona Lisa walked away.

Mona Lisa walked away,
right through the thick coat of dusty shellac,
out of the frame that disappeared
from the museum wall that had long preserved her.
As I stand before a canvas

pious tears flow copiously
and I have deep self-doubts.
I am a fake. And all this is a pity.
Ah, how pitiful the artist!
Mona Lisa walked away.

Mona Lisa walked away.
The one I paint is feeble, faint—
and canny.
By day, she seems an emerald,
by night, a ruby.
Blue like the lapis lazuli of Alexandria,
Mona Lisa walked away.

Mona Lisa walked away,
threatening my soul,
pouring oil on my burning passion,
a smile never leaving her lips.
Such envy I felt. Without weeping,
her face mysterious,
smiling through
her pale green pearly teeth
and stepping out of the frame,
Mona Lisa walked away.

Mona Lisa walked away.
It used to be I thought her so strange
that I would try to run away.
How very strange it all was!
How ravishing she was from behind,
and how forlorn I felt when she walked away,
vanishing like a phantom or a wisp of opium smoke.
Ah, that frosty last day of November when
Mona Lisa walked away.

In *Steps Along the Way*, Takamura's first collection of poems, the following note occurs: "I call a certain woman in the red-light district 'Mona Lisa'." This poem reflects his feelings at that time in his life, about 1909, when he returned from Europe and began to experience things that most boys experience in adolescence. Increasingly estranged from his family, he entered upon a decadent life and vigorously opposed social conventions of every kind. He fought against hypocrisy in his search for an authentic existence. He frequently drank with such writers in the Pan Society as Kitahara, Kinoshita, Yoshii and Nagata Hideo, and enjoyed much wild and drunken conviviality. For that group, such decadence represented a longing for a style of literary decadence, while Takamura actually immersed himself in unmitigated and bona fide decadence.

After a Pan meeting broke up one night in 1910, he went in a drunken state just to observe some of the girls on display in the house called Kawachirō in the red-light district. He was attracted by the hair style and features of one girl in particular whom he sketched on a pad that he kept in the breast of his kimono.

This girl, named Wakatayū, enchanted him so much that he visited her with great regularity; somewhat later she agreed to his proposal of marriage. Something of the Mona Lisa's mysterious smile moved on her face: "I had been used to wandering about and, probably unconsciously, looking for the archetypal woman I saw in my daydreaming. I met numerous women in my decadent daily wanderings." He found, at length, the "ideal" girl in Wakatayū. His quest was for the essence of femininity or the universal and eternal female. The Wakatayū in Kawachirō was the "doleful" representative who materialized before his eyes. On a day to day basis he was thoroughly decadent and yet in fact he was at the same time a dreamer. "Impressions of a Woman—My Dear Lover in Kawachirō"—is the title given to four short poems, one of which follows:

Ah, Kawachirō, my body and soul
find succor at the top of the stairs.
Looking at the curl of your lips, LA JOCONDE,
I can never fathom what you're feeling.

He found in Wakatayū—at last—the eternal woman, and after having "lost" her fell prey to a hopelessly uncontrollable grief. In the frequently reiterated "Mona Lisa walked away" his deep sadness reverberates. The real Mona Lisa of the painting and Wakatayū both had an enigmatic smile about them; but besides that the latter had a unique trill when she spoke. Her last words to him, the cold yet affectionate, "Be a good man!", are Mrs. Gioconda's ["a triumphant shogun's wife"]. Escaping the dusty varnish of the painting, escaping the frame, she entered his world. Yet no matter how worshipfully Kōtarō the "painter" sat in front of his canvas, she walked away, set free from her imprisonment within the walls of Kawachirō.

She was like an emerald by daylight; at night in her crimson Alexandria she was a blue gem. "Threatening my soul,/pouring oil on my burning passion." "Without weeping......smiling through her pale green pearly teeth," she walked away and he whispered to her how utterly attractive she was; and he went so far as to jot down that memorable date of 30th November.

This was to be their final encounter, a moment branded upon his mind; and yet in the very next year another Mona Lisa suddenly materialized—this time an innocent young woman rather than a scarlet woman. Her name was Naganuma Chieko and in her he discovered the very image of Wakatayū. He eventually married her and washed his hands of the decadent life.

To a Woman
(from *Selected Poems for Chieko*)

I can't bear for you
to go away—

Like a fruit before a blossom,
like a bud before the seed,
like spring just after summer—
don't do anything as unnatural as that.
It almost makes me cry
to think of a gracious woman
marrying a typical, ordinary man.
I can't stand to think
of a timid little bird like you,
a wild wind like you,
marrying at all.

I can't bear for you
to go away—

How can you do that so easily?
I don't know what to say—
How can you degrade yourself like that?
How can you do it?
It's meaningless giving yourself like that,
leaving yourself behind

and taking on public roles.
Marry a man like that?
I tell you, it's ridiculous;
it's a downright shame!
It's like one of Titian's women
going out shopping
in some mediocre place downtown.
It makes me sad and lonely.
It's like a big gloxinia
you gave me
that's withering
little by little.
It's like watching the gloxinia wither.
I'm watching you fly off
across the sky.
The waste of a wave that crashes and vanishes.
Transient, alone, my heart aches—
yet it's not love after all.
Holy Mary, it's not real love!
It's not!
I'm just speechless.
I can't bear for you
to go away—
not only that, but you're going to get married.
You're going to give your heart to another man.

The above poem, first published in a magazine, was entitled, "N—to a Woman.G" The initial denoted Naganuma Chieko, born in Fukushima Prefecture three years before Kōtarō's birth. After finishing a girls' high school in her hometown, she entered Japan Women's College to study home economics, and next enrolled in the Pacific Institute of the Fine Arts where she became a member of an organization called Seitō which in her time was a relatively radical organization devoted to "The New Woman". Their founder was Hiratsuka Raichō, who on account of her early work in feminism became very famous in Japan.

Kōtarō and Chieko first met in 1911. In a work called *Paragons* he referred to this meeting in words to the effect that instead of a cross, Chieko miraculously appeared in front of a hooligan." (from the poem "Decadence"). And (in "Living Beautifully") he further stated that "As a result of being purified by her, I finally found my true self." Their meeting, as is only obvious, was crucial in his life. In "To a Woman" the opening lines, "I can't bear for you/to go away—"remind one of a frustrated child asking for the impossible.

In her he found the archetypal" Eternal woman"by whose life he felt ennobled. That by her parents' decision she should leave to marry another man struck him as at once immoral and irrational. Such a noble woman resembling one of Titian's shopping in a seedy neighborhood he thought unimaginable.

His real feeling was, "It's not love." As far as love is concerned, *that* smacked of such lust as he experienced during his decadent period, and yet he insisted that his longing for her should have a spiritual basis. For all that, he truly wanted her. It was intolerable for him to think of her body at the mercy of another man. Here is a quatrain he wrote later (from "The Lascivious Heart"):

> Women are wanton.
> So am I.
> Tirelessly
> we shine with lust.

Love as lust is here unmistakable.

Two Beneath the Trees
—In Adachigahara, Tōhoku, under forked pines—
(from *Selected Poems for Chieko*)

Ah! Mt. Atatara!
And that shining is the Abukuma River.
As we sit beneath a pair of pines barely speaking,
half in and out of sleep,
a wind from the distant past blows blue-green.
Here at the onset of winter a great field spreads out before us
and flames of joy pass between us, hand to hand.
We shall not hide our joy behind that white cloud looking down on us.
A curious incense is glowing in your heart's burner.
Your hand miraculously guides me down to the ocean-bed of life.
In these now ten years I have found in you
the essence of the Eternal Woman.
I shall be cleansed of my romantic agony by the smoke
that curls around infinity
and the fountain of youth will fill my bitter cup.
And yet the intangible force that touches you, ever changing,
is outright evil.

Ah! Mt. Atatara!
And that shining is the Abukuma River.

This is where you were born.
You can see the small black and white vault
where your family ages sake.
Let's lie down and breathe in the good sweet scent, cool, pleasant,
slender and malleable—like you yourself.
Tomorrow I must take a long trip
to that venomous city swirling in love and hate.
I fear being again in the midst of that endless human comedy.
This is where you were born.
Heaven and earth produced this particular, strange flesh.
Wind still blows in the pines.
Tell me again about the melancholic lay of the land
Here, as winter begins.

That's Mt. Atatara.
That shining is the Abukuma River.

Written in 1923, nine years into their marriage, the poem's words "a decade we have walked together" suggest that he is reviewing their life together.

"Chieko," he wrote at that time, "[always] fell ill and [always] recovered upon returning to her hometown of Nihon Matsu-chō in Fukushima Prefecture. She stayed there almost half-a-year." She complained that she wanted to see a real sky, since Tokyo had none. Both the climate and the atmosphere of Tokyo went against her grain. "The real sky," she often said, "is the blue sky over Mt. Atatara." The sight of the "real sky" restored her health. There was in Chieko a pure savagery; an uncontrollable, wild beast dwelt within her. Kōtarō loved her beast-like, wild, innocent fury. He was enraptured by the fact that this "Clear, limpid, innocent creature lived, moved and desired."

A windfall of royalties from his translation work allowed him at this time to visit Chieko, who had long been staying with her parents. She guided him around her hometown with great delight. "One day we strolled through a pine grove behind her parents' house and sat on the edge of a cliff that commanded a panoramic view. Beyond the rice paddies we saw the white walls of her parents' winery and to the right, Mt. Atatara. That shining is the Abukuma River." This phrase is used three times in the poem and is reminiscent of the other-worldly. The two of them, holding hands and filled with passion, were transported by this edenic setting where pines were singing in the wind. Kōtarō was thinking less of the landscape than of "a woman's infinity" in the comfortable self-containment of herself in this landscape, which has been transformed by their rapture. She was utterly at one with this early winter landscape. Because she was a product of this landscape, it was for him no trifling matter. Like the landscape here in northern Japan, his love-life was a green wind among the scented pines, a pleasant touch of coolness.

SATŌ HARUO (1892-1964)

Song of the Saury
(from *My 1922*)

Autumn wind,
if you have a heart,
please tell this sad tale.
There was a man
sitting alone
eating saury for supper,
lost in his thoughts.

Saury, saury!
In his hometown people were used to
sprinkling green tangerine juice on their saury.
Thinking this custom odd but nice,
a woman was selecting some tangerines.
Now, pitifully, a half-abandoned wife,
a betrayed man, and at their side
a little girl, abandoned by her father,
is fumbling with little chopsticks, wanting
to ask the man if he please wouldn't eat the fish intestines.

Autumn wind,
you must look at this pitiful little unusual gathering
of people at supper.
Autumn wind,
how do you feel?
Please tell me at least

that this moment of supper-time
is not a dream.

Autumn wind,
if you have a heart,
please tell this sad tale
to a woman
whose husband has returned
and to a little girl
whose father is found.
There was a man eating saury for supper,
eating alone, and weeping.

Saury, saury!
Is it bitter or salty?
In what town are they used to dropping warm tears
on their saury as they eat?
Ah!
Isn't it strange wanting to ask myself such a question!

When autumn comes and saury are in season, all Japanese recall this poem. One of Satō's good friends was the novelist Tanizaki Jun'ichirō. Tanizaki and his wife Chiyoko had one child—a daughter—but this couple gradually became estranged; meanwhile, love began to blossom between Satō and Chiyoko, and indeed Tanizaki himself encouraged this relationship for a time. He soon changed his mind, however, and tried to rekindle his marriage with Chiyoko. So Satō had to stay away from them for six years. This poem was written in those years.

Later, Chiyoko and Satō got married. This development met with severe public censure and caused suffering to Haruo and Chiyoko. As I mentioned before, the poem was written when Satō was desperately longing for her. He explained later that at that time he would play plaintive melodies on an old flute. The poem's first two lines (lit., "Alas,/autumn wind") echo the old-fashioned folksong in which a woman who drifted away to Echizen in Fukui Prefecture asked an east wind to deliver her message; or she sang words to this effect: "I wish the wind would blow my words to... but...." This song comes from a book called *Ryōjin-Hishō* (Collection of Old Folk Ballads and Songs).

The second stanza recalls Kumano Shingū in Wakayama Prefecture—Satō's hometown—where there was a custom of eating saury sprinkled with the juice of green tangerines. Tanizaki Chiyoko knew his preferences well and always prepared tangerines for this purpose. The poem describes the evening meal at Tanizaki's home in Odawara, Tanizaki himself being absent. It is a strange scene, this "unusual gathering." The poet ardently appeals to the autumn wind in the saury season to witness and testify, in stanza three: the formerly precious, strange family gathering was *not* a dream.

In stanza two "a half-abandoned wife" and "betrayed man" reflect Chiyoko and Haruo's own broken marriage. "A little girl, abandoned by her father" occurs, which in stanza four will be reversed to read "a woman whose husband has returned/and a little girl whose father is found." A particular poetic sentiment broods in the lyric and epic aspects of the poem. Something like the deep, pathetic wailing of a violin suffuses the tone. [Trans.' note: Here Kenkichi tries to make us notice that this poem has an echo of Paul Verlaine's famous piece *"Autumn Song."]

In the final stanza he seems to have overcome his sorrow and reflected on it: "Isn't it strange wanting to ask myself such a question! "A tone of self-mockery is created. "…dropping warm tears" refers to "everyone's teardrops shed on dried rice" in "Azuma Kudari," part nine of the *Ise Monogatari* (*The Tale of Ise*), where the following situation occurs. Asked to compose a waka expressive of his feelings, Ariwara Narihira wrote down a feeling which is quite universal. When people heard it straight from the heart of a man, they all shed tears on their dried rice.

> I left my dear wife
> back in Kyoto
> and have come this long distance,
> and now I feel very sad
> and forlorn.

Tanizaki Jun'ichirō explained that he had no idea how to act during his six-years' break with Satō, because Satō clearly expressed his feelings about Chiyoko, unburdening himself utterly. He dedicated many poems to Chiyoko but the fact that a poem like this was printed meant that she could learn of his feelings. In this sense the poem served as a love letter.

> *With long sobs
> the violin-throbs

of autumn wound
my heart with languorous
and monotonous
sound.

Choking and pale
when I mind the tale
the hours keep,
my memory strays
down other days
and I weep;

and I let me go
where ill winds blow,
now here, now there,
harried and sped,
even as a dead
leaf, anywhere.

(Trans. C. F. MacIntyre)

MURŌ SAISEI (1889-1962)

Forbidden Flower
(from *Poems of Forgotten Spring*)

Should I fall in love with a married woman
I would no longer ache for young girls.
Some day you may feel the same.

In my mind's eye I still see his lonely face
as he said these words.
What he said rings true to me.
That other fellow's vibrant wife
is alluring,
because she is ripely beautiful and out of reach,
like a sad, drooping flower.
It is a savage illegality to love another man's wife
in this desolate world—savage, isn't it?

The "you" of the first stanza was probably Murō's friend Satō Haruo, for Haruo
burned with love for Tanizaki's wife Chiyoko at the time Murō wrote the poem,
as we have just seen.

As a result of Haruo's experience, Saisei reflected deeply on the awful law
that forbids one man to woo another man's wife. The law is surely inevitable,
because anther man's wife ("property") indeed was attractive.

In this poem Saisei speaks of a woman's sensuous beauty. He, too, worships
on his knees before a coquettishly refined beauty, all the more deeply because
she is "another man's property." He devotedly praises her physical
attractiveness because he takes Haruo's words too much to heart.

HAGIWARA SAKUTARŌ (1886-1942)

Passionate Love
(from *Howling at the Moon*)

A woman cleanly snips off blades of grass
with her pretty teeth.
Ah, you female!
I'll paint your whole face
with light blue grass ink
and inflame your lust.
Let's hide in the bushes and play!
Look!
Bellflowers are shaking their heads
and gentians are waving in the breeze.
I press against your breasts
and you answer with all your might.
Let's enjoy ourselves—this field is deserted—
you'll be my pet and we'll entwine like snakes,
slithering, coiling.
I'll smear your fair skin with the juice of green grass.

Sakutarō's first book of poems, *Howling at the Moon*, was prohibited from
being published because "Passionate Love" and "A Man in Love with Love"
were poems, it was said, that would encourage social demoralization.
Governmental education authorities at the time found such phrases as "inflame
your lust," "I press against your breasts" and "we'll entwine like snakes" to be
highly immoral.

Yet the poet's diction is, strangely enough, devoid of reality. True, we can see in the poem a decadent emotion, but the poet is not so much describing his personal experience as creating a "mood." He explained elsewhere that he aimed at "creating the atmosphere of heightened sexual desire or the beauty of that desire."

This poem is very sensual and yet he doesn't necessarily maintain that sensual ecstasy is the first principle of poetry. There is at least a longing for transport (Eros) at the base of this poem and it is in the idea of longing that the reality of a woman is to be found. The poem is at once sado-erotic and platonic.

HORIGUCHI DAIGAKU (1892-1981)

Memories
(from *A New Path*)

Many women wept for me,
though I no longer remember them.
Facets of their faces resolve
into one weeping face
in the cigarette smoke of a tedious day.
It hovers like a ghost in a movie.
I am moved, as in a melodrama.

One woman lives in Mexico—
her son
resembles me.
Through her copious tears
she tells her son,
'Your father died
before you were born.'

A second is a pious Spaniard
who is now patronized by a rich old man.
She has pasted my photo on the back of the crucifix
that hangs on her bedroom wall.
In her great piety she never forgets
her morning and evening prayers.

A third languidly gazes at the teeth marks
I left on her white skin

and is—as usual—lost in reverie
recalling the past.

The fourth has a large N
tattooed beside her left breast.
To a man who asks
what this N recalls, she answers,
'Why should I remember that?'

Many women wept for me,
though I no longer remember them.

Horiguchi enrolled in the Liberal Arts College of what is now Keio University
and lived a slothful life along with Satō Haruo. Shortly he was summoned to
live with his father who was filling a diplomatic post in Mexico. Later he
traveled to Belgium, Switzerland, Spain, Rumania, France, and other European
and American cities. He was abroad from his early twenties into his early
thirties.

There are no sweet memories set down in this poem in which he recalls his
encounters with women. His passion flags as he expresses, ironically, the
feeling that the face "hovers like a ghost in a movie./I am moved, as in a
melodrama."

Women come and go incessantly in his flippant, wanton and desperate way
of speaking, and yet behind the light tone run a melancholy and an ennui
informed by a sense of life as empty and lonely. As witty as the poem may be,
it exudes a bitter, forlorn element. Weak of body and suspecting that he would
die young, he sings out an old man's feelings as an expression of his youthful
nihilism. He lacks the deep emotions of a man truly in love with life. But we
must admit that the lightness here serves the poem's purposes well.

ŌTE TAKUJI (1887-1934)

Love
(from *Indigo Toad*)

My love is the face of the setting sun on the water.
My love is a thought of a leaf falling at midnight.
Wordless, voiceless and without shadows.

This brief poem alludes to a secret love of Takuji's. The poem is silent on the identity of the "face" and the "leaf." The three adjectives suggest a fading away, as of something to be hidden, something very faint, something he carefully kept to himself.

It is in his own internal thoughts that his love poems are completed, the flame of love now burning now extinguished in the privacy of his heart; however, such a brief, tenuous feeling is exquisitely lyricized.

Takuji died in 1934 in Nangoin, a sanitorium in Chigasaki. In fact, before she became an actress, Yamamoto Yasue used to work for the same firm as the poet. She quit and joined the new style (Western) drama troupe. The poet, it is said, secretly conceived an affection for her and yearned for her all his life. Although love for her is an undercurrent in his love poems, she evidently knew nothing of his feelings. Another of his poems reads:

Phantasmagoria
(from *Indigo Toad*)

You, in sunlight, are a totally tottering flower.
You, out of earshot, are a fish with a most indistinct voice.
Your heart is dripping.
You trip over your tongue.
You are pale, piling dream on dream.
You float and drift on the water
and summon the distant silence at twilight.

You are an invisible light at sea.
You are pistil and stamen endlessly regenerated.
You are visible;
You are invisible.
You are, tottering in all your glory, always on my mind.

When a turquoise vision visits me
I drift off, I don't know where,
and immerse myself deep in dreams.
Like an unending fine snow
my mind flows and floats,
faintly playing on the lips of Death.

You are a blurred shadow walking along no road.
The shadow grows lustrous and entangled;
it is gently blown.

Stanzas one, two and four provide various images of the indescribable phantasmagoric "you"; stanza three takes account of the mind of "I....playing on the lips of Death" after drifting off, while dreaming of the phantasmagoric "you." With no place to go, afloat in empty air, helpless love is dwelt upon at length.

When I consider that this poet lived the fullest yet emptiest life, nourishing a vision to the very last, I feel how very very different the age is in which we live now.

MIYOSHI TATSUJI (1900-1964)

A Grass Hermitage
(from *A Flower Basket*)

An honored guest in a grass hermitage:
a white cotton rose in a sunlit garden.
Being profoundly stirred,
my heart roars like the sea.

Peach Blossoms

From the dark sky snow falls and falls
on pitiful peach blossoms in the backyard,
which makes me think
there is no tomorrow.

A Distant Mountain

Spring has arrived from a distant mountain
and great white blossoms of the cucumber tree spread out overhead.
A cloud comes back. But I must travel on
going—where, I wonder?

A Passer-By

A passer-by takes notice
of the small white blossoms of the spindle tree
and moves on. But I see, hidden behind the tree,
a woman's white face.

Too Voluptuous

Too voluptuous,
a white peony in a vase.
The sight wounds me.
Who understands my heart?

Miyoshi moved to Mikuni in Fukui Prefecture in March, 1944. The dwelling, a two-story cottage fronting on the Sea of Japan, belonged to a friend. The roar of the sea was constant in his rooms. He intended to marry a beautiful woman.

Back in 1926 when Hagiwara Sakutarō was staying in Magome Village in the Ebara district of Tokyo, his younger sister Ai, who was twice divorced, lived with him for a while. The young poet Tatsuji frequently visited and at length found himself in love with her. In response to his proposal she rejected him, because he was still a penniless student.

She went on to marry the poet Satō Sōnosuke. In May 1942 her brother Sakutarō died and then suddenly, just four days later, so did her husband. Tatsuji now fanned back into flame the love he had borne her over a period of sixteen years, and so he rented the Mikuni house and awaited her arrival.

This story came to light only later when Sakutarō's daughter Yōko published a partial biography of Miyoshi entitled *Blossoms in the Heavens Above* following his death. The Miyoshi-Ai relationship soon deteriorated; she left him the following March. But be that as it may, *A Flower Basket* is a brief sequence of love poems dedicated to Ai. One of Miyoshi's favorite followers—Ishihara Yatsuka—points out that Miyoshi inserted numerous favorite flowers in his poems as motifs. *A Flower Basket* was published in May; she arrived in June; therefore the poems are redolent of the love he long bore her and, though somewhat restrained, the feeling is that of a man who at last expected fullness of love.

The "honored guest" of "A Grass Hermitage" is of course Ai; yet in "Peach Blossoms," which contains no obvious longing for any woman, the" pity"suggests longing. In those early days of the war people suspected that tomorrow might never come and so all the more did it seem that red peach blossoms were irreplaceably beautiful.

"A Distant Mountain" is excellently compact. White blossoms are dazzling in the spring of the north country like heavenly flowers. At the end of the road in the Hokuriku district, this rented home appears to be his final dwelling place, now steeped in deep melancholy. Although he awaits his love, what strikes him very strongly is the reverse side of joy, namely, sorrow.

By "the small white blossoms of the spindle tree" he indicates a centrifugal blossoming as well as a woman's graceful visage.

And "a white peony in a vase" suggests his longing for a simple life. He questions whether it is after all inappropriate to receive her in his poor cottage. But he suppresses his feelings.

Woodpecker
(from *Hometown Flowers*)

Woodpecker
Woodpecker
. . . .

From the treetop I am pointing at
it suddenly vanishes into the woods.
. . . .

You, my love,
you must have seen it, too.
. . . .

Red-breasted,
singing plaintively,
that shadowy bird.
. . . .

I don't want you,
even you with your cold heart,
to forget what we've seen today:
. . . .

Human
grief
unfathomable

. . . .

that shadowy bird
suddenly vanishing
into the woods.

. . . .

Listen—
the wind's voice,
bird song here and there.

. . . .

Soon
this road will separate us.

. . . .

Trees are bare,
the moon waxes.

. . . .

Only a few leaves
flutter down.

One November day Tatsuji and Ai quarreled, as this poem suggests. He apparently realized that they were incompatible and determined to end their relationship. Not until the following March, however, did he act, because his affection for her somehow remained. The poem nonetheless indicates that in his heart he has already reached his decision.

Bearing in mind the likelihood of a split, they calmly discussed the matter. Looking at the lone red-breasted woodpecker, hearing its song, Tatsuji seems to project upon the bird his own feelings, thus arousing in her a feeling of tenderness. He asks for her understanding of "Human grief" by calling up the eternally singing bird with its flaming heart, even though he is aware of her cold-heartedness.

Having nurtured his affection for her for nearly two decades, he was at a loss as to how to manage his feelings. A chilly wind swept through his heart. The poem's imagery obviously foreshadows the ultimate separation. Although he knows about her coldness he wishes that she would never forget this day. The one thing he can do is express his heartrending hope, which in fact is, in other words, rooted unmistakably in his painful love for her.

NAKAHARA CHŪYA (1907-1937)

Song Sung by a Cuckolded Husband
(from *Songs of Bygone Days*)

You love me;
    never hated me.

I love you, too;
    it's my destiny.

Two souls fell in love unawares,
    love long since habitual.

And yet we both badly want to have fun
elsewhere.

The natural feeling of love seems sometimes
an impediment.

Our love smells more of a hospital
    than of a delicious perfume,

Where the most intimate people sometimes
hate each other most intensely.

Later we find ourselves immersed
in a nameless remorse.

Ah, our wanton hearts
blind us to the Truth.

Not a delicious perfume
but the hospital's subtle, alluring scent.

The love triangle involving Chūya, Hasegawa Yasuko and Kobayashi Hideo, which the latter referred to as "cooperation through hatred," seems almost unimaginable.

At seventeen Chūya transferred from a hometown school in Yamaguchi Prefecture to Kyoto's Ritsumeikan High School. He met the runaway Hasegawa who hoped to be a movie star. They lived together and the next year moved to Tokyo. It wasn't a year before she abandoned him in order to live with Kobayashi. In one book Chūya remarked, "Ever since that time I have been terribly chagrined." Kobayashi and Nakahara became alienated for a time. According to Ōoka Shōhei's *Songs of Bygone Days*, "A runaway girl's anxiety seemed to have resulted in her over-dependence on Kobayashi or in her flirtatiousness with other men. So Kobayashi and Chūya had a long talk."

In three years' time Kobayashi himself fled from the hysterical Yasuko, taking refuge in Nara Prefecture. Once again Chūya invited her to live with him—and she flatly refused. She bore the child of a leftist student, became a new face in the cinema world, married a rich man and persuaded him to establish the Nakahara Chūya Award for poetry.

Whether detailed prying into the biographical facts would be helpful in our appreciating Chūya's poetry there is no way of knowing, and yet the sexual triangle does inevitably lie behind the above poem. It's easy to say that he loved Yasuko but no one can truly know for certain; since they themselves could not clarify their feelings, we have no choice but to accept his poem at face value, in which sense, then, we see a mutually-held deep love, though in some curious way they "sometimes hate each other most."

The corrupt, decadent flesh cast a shadow on a noble spiritual love. They occasionally took pleasure more in the subtle odor of the hospital than in the scent of perfume.

Both their love and their hatred are aspects of their karma. Being cuckolded was a matter of great shame. His heart replete with bitter thoughts, he nonetheless kept on patiently cultivating his love for her. Thus Chūya's poetry.

YAMANOGUCHI BAKU (1903-1963)

My Visit's Purpose
(from *The Poems of Yamanoguchi Baku*)

What would you say
if I were to come
to visit your daughter?

What further would you say if I said
I'd come all the way to Hatagaoka
for that purpose?

If—just if—
my iffy story were true,
what, madam, would you say?

That girl so beautifully blooming. . . .
that girl so beautifully blooming. . . .
only when I see the truth do I drink green tea this slowly.

The poet's ostensible purpose is to visit the girl's mother, yet his poem's frequent" ifs"declare his real purpose, which of course makes us smile. The following—a pastoral waka from the *Man'yōshū*—is a case in point:

Horribly scolded by your mother,
I must go now.
But before I do,
my love, please, hurry out here,
like the blue behind the clouds. (#3519)

Baku's poem is similar to the *Man'yōshū* waka and would be even more so if this amiable, ill-mannered man were to be reprimanded by the mother.

Of course Baku couldn't tell the mother so boldly what his intention was and so instead he expressed his sentiments and frustration in the form of this poem. The style of the poem is enlivened by the simple metaphor of the girl as a blossoming flower.

ITŌ SHIZUO (1906-1953)

Elegy for a Living Loved One
(from *Elegy for a Living Loved One*)

The sun shines gloriously—
or at least I hope it will.

We've quietly walked along,
hands held tightly.
Whatever the reason for this,
I think there surely is
some inner sense that searches for, feels, purity.
Birds are always singing,
trees and flowers endlessly whispering,
even for those who don't perceive the beauty.
You and I now listen
purposefully, willingly, to their magnificent hymns.
Ah, my darling,
inside this brilliant sunshine
there lurks a silent emptiness.
There would be no point
in the eye's perceiving such a thing.
Useless!
I climb the deserted mountain
and let the sun I have long hoped for
shine out again across the barren lake of me.

Itō had in his Saga High School days a teacher named Sakai Yasutarō who
hailed from Isahaya, a town in Nagasaki, where Itō also came from. Just as Itō
entered Kyoto University, Sakai was transferred to a high school in Kobe near
Kyoto. Whenever some important matter came up, Itō visited Sakai at length.
He was attracted to Sakai's two daughters, Yasuyo and Yuriko. When the elder
sister married, he directed all his loving attention to Yuriko. Itō was, however,
hopelessly saddled with debts incurred by his deceased father and so he would
never marry. His mood became increasingly stoic, with an undercurrent of
despair.

"The sun shines gloriously—." He begins this poem in the present tense, but
immediately changes to the future in "...I hope it will." He deals not with the
present reality but with his hope. The fourth line's "hands held tightly" may
betoken his being at a loss for words while also possibly suggesting the
intensity of his hope. In his strolling he seems drawn by an unseen force;
perhaps he is fantasizing or even willing" hope"into existence in the process of
the ʲ"magnificent hymns" of sun, birds, trees and flowers.

Thus his "Ah, my darling!" actually finds him alone on the deserted mountain
in bright sunshine. The icy sun is reflected all across the lake that seems to him
all but lifeless. The scenery is frozen by the deep grief of loneliness. This is

doubtless more an elegiac poem bespeaking fruitless memory than it is a real love poem.

II

Death and Life

Love poems and elegies are two of the principal kinds of poems found in the *Man'yōshū*. Indeed our greatest and unchanging human experiences are of love and death.

In Japanese, "elegy"originally referred to the singing of a dirge as a funeral hearse was being pulled along by mourners. The modern meaning is also that of a poem lamenting a person's death.

But in the *Man'yōshū* there are also elegies in which the poet focusses exclusively on his own troubles. There is one, for instance, by Prince Arima pitying his personal fate while looking at gnarled pine branches (gnarls symbolizing good luck in the *Man'yōshū* period).

Another such elegy, by Kakinomoto-no-Hitomaro, expresses grief over the writer's exile to Iwami Province. This type of elegy later becomes known as "Jisei no Uta"(poems that anticipate sorrowfully one's own death or lament bad luck). They were sometimes called "Jisei no Hokku"(death haiku). Of course some writers were, and some were not, certain of the day of their death.

Let us inspect some modern "death poems."

MASAOKA SHIKI (1867-1902)

Though the gourd blossoms,
phlegm has gathered.
I shall become a buddha.

An ocean of phlegm
has gathered.
The gourd juice comes too late.

When the juice was at its prime
two days ago
they failed to collect it.

Shiki wrote these three haiku the day before he died. He grew gourds in the garden of his tiny hut, the watery juice therefrom said to have been an effective expectorant. His gourds, however, were late blooming and so, the fruit not yet ready, phlegm collected in a great glob in his throat. There is a touch of humor in his calling himself a buddha [Trans.' note: in Buddhism it is believed that at their death all creatures become buddhas but at the same time the Adam's apple in Japanese is the "throat buddha"—because of its resemblance to a buddha's face carved out of stone or wood]. In all really good haiku a touch of humor is present.

The hyperbole of "an ocean of phlegm" also amuses. The Japanese phrase for the amount of phlegm reads "sixteen liters." This alludes to the Chinese poet Li Po's consumption of sixteen liters of wine while composing his famous one-hundred poems (according to Li Po's fellow-poet Tu Fu's explanation). The reality of approaching death disturbs him into writing, as it were, out of desperation, yet he remains rather lucid. Also amusing is the ironic "The gourd juice comes too late."

August 15th on the old calendar was said to be the best day for the drinking of gourd juice, but his wife's constant attendance upon Shiki prevented her from collecting the juice on that day.

Writers of death haiku were apt to pretend indifference to their death, in contrast to the seriousness with which ancient poets faced their death. Shiki's haiku does not particularly pose in that way; instead, he reacts quite objectively and comes up with an attractive light-heartedness.

KAWABATA BŌSHA (1900-1941)
(from *The Collected Haiku of Kawabata Bōsha*)

The magnolia petals are falling.
I wonder,
Where am I going?

By the well of loneliness,
wakened by thunder:
'Oh! I'm still alive!'

This summer
my arm grows even thinner,
weaker, heavier.

Lying on my stony pillow,
I feel myself joining in
the shower of cicada-song.

Bōsha died on July 17th, having been by birth poorly constituted. In the late 1920's he contracted tuberculosis and from that time on was almost always in bed. Writing haiku seemed the only choice open to him.

The four above are evidently the last ones he ever wrote, but we are not certain that he knew they would be his death haiku. Fukagawa Shōichirō, the editor of Bōsha's collected haiku, stated that the first haiku given above truly contains the poet's desire to leave this world. Instead of the usual touch of humor found in Shiki's poems, there emerges some ghastly element in Bōsha's haiku. A magnolia grew in front of Bōsha's hut. The haiku alludes to the Buddhist rite of a procession of people scattering tiny paper lotus petals while intoning verses from a sutra. The Chinese characters literally mean "falling petals." It is an expression that was also used of such violent deaths as were often met in the Second World War.

A falling petal seemed, just as Bōsha himself thought, bound for no destination. Aware of his imminent death, he deliberately used the term "falling petals."

In the next haiku he speaks out of the depths of his loneliness, the thunder standing for the present reality that he is yet alive.

In the third he finds his strength and weight decreasing. His arm is like a small iron rod.

In the last, his pillow has grown "hard"and he hallucinates a bit, thinking himself one of the cicada whose screeching fills his room. It is the din of the cicada that dissolves into a "stony pillow."

TAKAMURA KŌTARŌ

Elegy, with Lemon
(from *Selected Poems for Chieko*)

You'd been waiting so long for a lemon.
Lying on your sad, bright white death bed,
you took it from me
and gnawed it with your beautiful teeth.
The aroma of topaz filled the air.

A few drops of juice from heaven
startled you back to sanity.
You faintly smiled through clear blue eyes.
You clenched my hand with a fistful of strength.
Though there was a storm in your throat,
at this life's last moment
you became Chieko again
and in that moment re-newed your life-long love.
For a while you breathed deeply
as once you had atop a mountain.
And then you stopped.
In the shade of cherry blossoms in front of your photograph
I shall once again today place a lemon, shining coolly, shining brightly.

It was October 1938 when Chieko died. It was she who saved him from drowning in his own decadence at an earlier time in his life. After several years' immersion in gloom she died a schizophrenic. In his essay "The Last Half of Chieko's Life" he states that "A few hours before she died she took the lemon I bought her and held it to her mouth. Seeing that, I felt washed body and soul by the comforting scent and refreshing juice of that fruit." The poem has it merely that she "gnawed it" with her beautiful teeth, which is a fresh and sensuous expression indeed.

For Chieko those drops of juice, truly a gift "from heaven," conjure up the image of her "clear blue eyes." She grasped his hand and died in a moment's revival of her "life-long love." This was a moment of exultation as she stood on the very edge between life and death. It was, as well, the exultation of love as symbolized in the aroma of a single lemon. Sick abed, she was yet full of life. Even in the moment when she returned to her normal, sane self, we can hear in her throat her death rales. She became the essential Chieko, bodying forth a brilliance beyond reality: a revelation of love. He recalled the nobility of her character as he had seen it when they climbed the mountain together.

The words "atop a mountain" are repeatedly used in his poems to express her pure animality. In another poem about a" weasel's scythe"[Trans.' note: the term for a cut in the skin caused by exposure to the vacuum formed by a cyclone]—a poem called "Purity" in *Beast Poems* —he states: "She inhaled the air of the mountain atop steep craggy cliffs and rode on the wind gusting up from the valley." The pure weasel slash was nothing but the incarnation of her wild spirit. Her figure as she breathed the pure air atop that mountain overlapped with her dying figure as breathed that air once more. And then her breathing stopped.

Is there another poem that so precisely captures a woman's beauty as she stands on the brink? It comes as a result of Kōtarō's aptness for encapsulating the far edges of human life. Or, I should say, the responsibility was Chieko's, for she pulled him back from confusion; and so it is Kōtarō who bows to her superiority.

A statue of two nude young girls facing each other stands by Lake Towada. This was sculptured by Kōtarō. The bodies are those of models; the faces are Chieko's as she lives in his heart.

YOSHINO HIDEO(1902-1967)

"A White Amaryllis"
(from *The Tanka of Yoshino Hideo*)

In the summer of 1944 my wife Hatsuko had pain in her stomach and was hospitalized in the Sato Surgery in Kamakura. She was never mobile again. She died on August 29th at age forty-two, leaving four children. My mentor, the tanka poet Aizu Yaichi, kindly gave her the posthumous Buddhist name of "Hatsu, Buddha's Vestal Virgin."

Amid fleas
leaping about,
your soul's cord
shrivels
and shrivels.

Your medicine gone,
I go
to buy
Government-made
Emergency Elixir of Life.

At morning I rise,
eager to succor her,
but am crestfallen when cicadas
bid farewell
to daylight.

Although you'll die
in a few days,
you lie abed
mending
a child's garment.

Searchlights
cross swords
in the sky.
The issue here is
already decided.

In the autumnal
deep of night,
the wind's fingers
seem to touch
your face.

Under cosmetics,
your swollen face
resembles
the face of
the Buddha's disciple.

I pray before your mortuary tablet,
but am still
spellbound
by
your husky, erotic voice.

Dead drunk,
I go
looking for
you
in the futon closet.

In the field
my children,
sowing wheat

for god and country,
will miss their mother.

Nirvana

On the brink
of death
you smile,
satisfied
with your life.

You pity me
for outliving you
and,
your breathing labored,
caress my hair.

Even
on the verge of death
you struggle
to summon
your last lust.

For the last time,
my love,
you ask for
the fire
of my love.

I am depressed,
but,
oblivious to the consequences,
shake
violently.

Among tanka treating his wife's death are numerous truly wrenching elegies.
The last three above are unprecedented in dealing with sex just before death.

They are solemn. And there is no room for beautifying or worrying over the subject. Even pleasure is missing as they come together.

As a last lunging after the source of life or for the combination of pitiful affection, they copulated. The pitifulness, loneliness and transience of life beneath the tanka strike home. Thus their experience clearly illustrates the phrase, "One life, one meeting," recognizing that everything is a unique event. Such tanka do not come easily, for after all to write poems of this sort requires great courage, a courage that enables one to confront the sudden truth of life.

MIYAZAWA KENJI (1896-1933)

The Morning of Eternal Farewell
(from *Spring and Asura*)

Before the day ends,
my sweet sister, you're going far away.
Sleet is falling this strangely bright day.
("Get me some sleet, will you?")
Wet sleet is falling
out of the faintly bright gloomy clouds.
("Get me some sleet, will you?")
Holding these two old patterned rice bowls
I get up and rush out
into the falling sleet
like a wobbling bullet
to catch some sleet for you to eat.
("Get me some sleet, will you?")
Sleet slops down
out of the pale leaden clouds.
Ah, Toshiko,
you ask me for sleet
because you hope to cheer me up
even as you lie
dying.
Thank you, my wonderful sister.
I'll follow a straight path, like you.
("Get me some sleet, will you?")
Gasping,
feverish,

you ask for a last bowl of sleet.......
falling from this world we call
galaxy, sun, atmosphere or somewhere.......
Sleet is falling in loneliness
on the two granite rocks.
Standing uncertainly on the rocks
I reach up to the lustrous pine branches
coated with the two-phased snow and water
and collect your final food,
these clear, cold droplets,
my dear, dear sister.
You will say farewell to these
familiar indigo rice bowls.
("Me...me...going by myself.")
You're actually going away.
You lie in the closed-off room
behind the dark folding screen
in the mosquito netting,
burning gently, palely.
Oh, my wonderful sister,
wherever I choose to scoop up sleet
it is everywhere pure white.
This beautiful sleet has come
out of this horrible, disturbed sky:
("When I come into the world again
I'll try not to worry only about myself.")
Before these two bowls of sleet
I deeply pray that they will become
bowls in 'Tusita heaven'
and that to you and all others
they will bring holy sustenance.
This I pray in all humility.

This poem comes from the series "Voiceless Lamentation" that the poet wrote deploring the death of Toshiko, two years his junior. She died on 27th November 1922, at the age of twenty-five. A bright woman, she deeply understood her brother and so her death was the deepest possible source of sorrow for him. Besides this poem, he wrote the two other poems "Pine Needles" and "Voiceless Lamentation" on the day she died. Given only one day to live, she asked him for some sleet, which he took to be her way of easing his anxiety. He was moved that in the throes of her own death agony she could trouble to think about his future. He then vowed to live as honorable a life as she had: his words "like you" suggest that, however briefly, her life had been upright. Because of his rich culturation, one finds terms from astronomy, meteorology and geology frequently cropping up in his poems. The term "two-phased," for instance, indicates sleet as a state of both solid and liquid. His reference to the gathering of her "final food" is exceptionally piously expressed. Sleet piled in the indigo Chinese bowls is so beautifully white that it will be transformed into heavenly sustenance, like manna, and will nourish all.

"Tusita heaven" is one of the six Buddhistic heavens of desire and is noted for a cloisonné palace where the Buddha Miroku lives. Outside the palace is an arcadia where all living things can enjoy untold pleasure. This is probably where Toshiko was bound.

Her northern Iwate dialect occurs in the poem, but the words are considered to be said by heavenly voices. The dialectic *Ame-juju* (sleet) occurs four times in the poem and seems to turn as she says it into a transparent, almost other-worldly, voice. Kenji's love for his sister is crystallized in this dirge.

Mr. Nakamura Tōru points out that Takamura Kōtarō must have written "Elegy, with Lemon" under the sway of this poem.

SAITŌ MOKICHI

My Deceased Mother
(from *Red Radiance*)

In my memory
broad leaves are glittering,
fluttering in the wind;
so, too, my heart,
unsettled, uneasy.

I am struck
suddenly
by the memory of seeds
that remain between those petals
of the white wisteria not yet fallen.

I feel urgently
that I must
once more
see my mother in distant Tōhoku
while she still lives.

She is near death
as I lie sleepless next to her.
The rice paddies stretch far and wide;
the croaking of the frogs
reaches the high dark heavens.

Two swallows
expose their vermilion throats
in the roof rafters
where they nest.
My dear, dear mother is dying.

A tiny green silkworm,
new-born,
wriggles across
young leaves of the oak
that flutter in sunlight.

Under a starry sky
the great leaves
that cover
my mother's corpse
burn red, burn fiercely.

In the morning
after her cremation
I noticed that medicinal weeds
and thistles around the crematory
have also been burned.

As I go along
the mountain path
the tree leaves

make mirages
and buds abound.

Parting the bamboo grass
with my hands
as I walk across the field,
I think I may be
searching for my mother.

In the distant dale
a bright crimson fire
brings back
the sad, painful memory
of my mother.

My spirit sinks
when I remember what they say
about those distant clouds
that float across the heavens:
that they are lifeless.

One of the highlights of *Red Radiance* consists of the two sections "Ohiro" and
"My Deceased Mother."

Mokichi's mother, Iku, died in Kanehei Village in Minami-Mudayama District
in Yamagata Prefecture on 23rd May 1913. Upon receiving the news of her
grave condition, he left Tokyo at once to be with her. His grief and anxiety lend
a certain subtlety to his words, "broad leaves" and "white wisteria" petals in the
prefatory tanka of this section. The petals fall but some yet remain, among
which one can see pod-shaped seeds.

Such expressions as "near death" and "vermilion throats" are the crowning
heart's grief of the series. Mokichi later on explains that he was thinking of
Buddha's death scene where Buddha in the center is surrounded by disciples,
demi-gods and others, all weeping. And he receives a deep Buddhist impression
when the swallows begin to nest inside the house where his mother lies dying.
The open-billed crimson throats are the finishing touch on this Buddhist
painting. The tanka centering on silkworms represents an actual sighting as
Mokichi walked to the crematory. He had been familiar since childhood with
such worms which he here had no trouble spotting. In a book he authored
entitled *Four Decades of Writing Tanka* he states that "A crematory is a shallow

hollow in a paddy surrounded by a stone wall. We blanketed the coffin with twigs and straw and set it afire. By daybeak the fire had finally burned itself out." One visualizes the progress of a plain, simple country cremation.

After the cremation Mokichi went to relax for two nights at the Takayu hot springs. When he" goes along"the mountain the movement is not merely of his feet; it is also a bearing up under his sadness.

(from *Aratama*)

Ah, the living go away.
In the distance
in the vale
the sound of coldness
in the giant cedar.......

I go against
the wind-blasted cold
and in the distance
a crow
cries.

These two tanka come from the series "My Grandmother," written when she died. Her name was Hide. The word" go"is conspicuous and implies that" all things flow; are not static'—a common Japanese idea. He probably has in mind this waka from the *Man'yōshū* which is echoed in his own tanka:

It's been a long time
since you went away.
I shall go up the mountain
to meet you, and wait
and wait.

Although this is officially a love poem it is actually a dirge. The indication is probably that a lover visits her deceased mate on the mountain, thus piously evoking the soul of the dead. His visit to the mountain as recorded in the foregoing tanka is not unrelated to the ideas of ancient dirges found in the

Man'yōshū. The rusticity of the *Man'yōshū* waka suggests that in all probability there is a direct kinship between it and Mokichi's tanka.

MURŌ SAISEI

Elegy
(from *Till the Death of a Girl*)

You should be under the bontan tree.
'Bontan'—and tears begin.
Bontan died in distant Kagoshima.
Nine-year-old Bontan.
Her eyes were pearls.
Bontan, loved by all.
'A-B-C-D-E-F-G...'
Ah! 'H-I-J-K....'
Her lovely hand has gone far away
looking for her mother in heaven.
Your grandpa
is on his way to the 'sparrows' abode!
'Is Fujiko here?
Is Fujiko here, by any chance?'

This short poem appears in Saisei's autobiographical novel. Still young and with no reputation, he found boarding in Yanaka in Tokyo. Next door a pretty little girl named Yamamoto Fujiko lived. She felt very friendly towards him. They met briefly every day. Since her parents were from Kagoshima the girl often spoke of the fruit famous in those parts called "bontan"(pomelo, or shaddock). So he began calling her "Bontan."

It happened that about the time that Fujiko's family returned to Kagoshima, Saisei went to his hometown of Kanazawa. Some two months later Saisei received a letter from Fujiko's father in which her death was announced. The news reduced him to profound tears.

During the desolate cold days of his bleak experience in Yanaka, Fujiko had been for him a "little savior" Upon reading the letter he placed palm to palm and prayed for her soul, and then wrote the poem. After the fashion of a nursery rhyme, it is a fit tribute to the innocent girl. The poem's words and the lack of a consistently unified style all the more befit the theme.

The "should" of the first line reveals his strong hope that she was buried beneath the tree by whose name he called her. In repetition the tree's name by turns becomes her nickname. The A-B-C lines recall her having read her elementary school reader to Saisei and here he seems to grow speechless and to reach an emotional peak. The enquiring, "Is Fujiko here?" stands for those numerous times when they played and talked together, as well as echoes a line from a grade school song based on a famous folktale [Trans.' note: about a grandfather who is looking in the woods for the abode of a sweet little sparrow whose tongue was rudely cut out by a greedy old woman].

Saisei seems completely distraught; however, his aching affection, threaded throughout the poem, is close to love. We may scruple to call this a true love poem, yet we may readily call it a dirge for a loved one, thoroughly steeped in grief.

That he deeply sympathized with the young, the poor, the weak and the oppressed is clear. He was sympathetically reading Dostoevski at the time. Such sympathy finds good form in his collection *Poems of Love*.

SHAKU CHŌKŪ (1887-1953)

"The Sulfurous Island"
(from *Japanese Man*)

(His last note to me as the war progressed—I think he could have written more. I pray somehow he'll keep alive, minute by minute.)

The February moon
is deep
in the distance.
I wonder if my son still lives,
fighting?

Longing for my son
far off on that Pacific island,
I unconsciously
pat my fatherly head
for comfort and in perplexity.

Facing towards
that distant war-torn island,
I cannot but
visualize my son and me
sleeping peacefully.

(from "The Sounds of Silence")

My son having travelled
far beyond those massive clouds,
I soothe my nerves
by reminding myself
there's nothing I can do.

I wonder
if there will come a time
when I demand
my honored dead son
return to me alive.

I will not
speak of
the dream I had,
because
it is so impoverishing.

(from "That Day......Might Come")

The name of a certain courtier
who died
in the service of his prince
comes back to me
and never leaves me.

Though it is hard
to conceive of my son's dying,

it
could indeed
happen.

As I envision the return
of my son's remains
I grieve
in the painful knowledge
of how terribly brief life has been.

Even though
our sons return to us
dead,
there would be some comfort
in comforting each other.

(from "Finally, No Return")

No trace remains
of my son
and now
step by step
a broken nation disarms.

It was in 1928 that Shaku Chōkū (real name, Origuchi Shinobu) began living with Fujii Harumi, his pupil, in Ōimachi, Tokyo. Fujii was then a student at Kokugakuin. This young man continued for sixteen years to care for his master with unfailing modesty. A wooden gate in front of his parents' house in Ichinomiya, on the Noto Peninsula, is frequently referred to by Chōkū in his tanka.

In 1944 this young man was drafted as a lieutenant and was sent to Iwo Jima. Chōkū, having seriously considered the matter, legally adopted Fujii. On 4th February 1945 the American Army landed on Iwo Jima. Fujii's whereabouts were officially a secret but through one letter Chōkū realized where he was. As the fierce fighting approached a conclusion, Chōkū dwelt intensely on the matter, filled unceasingly with anxiety. The first tanka above clearly reflects his agony.

The following poem (a chōka, or long poem) of the same period equally reflects his anxiety:

Father Island, Mother Island
(from *Modern Elegies*)

Mother Island with the sagging breasts.
Father Island, hold him to your breast.

Father and Mother Islands stand
in the vast South Pacific.

I look at
these islands longingly
and say,

"Hear my prayer, Mother Island:
'Protect our son.' So be it!"

This poem is a prayer representing the feelings of all parents for all sons who were defending Iwo Jima, but is, more particularly, based on the stern reality that Chōkū's own Harumi was one of those. "Protect our son. So be it!" is every parent's heartfelt wish. In March 1945 the Japanese Army's press division reported that all soldiers died honorably defending Iwo Jima. Hence, thought Chōkū, the end had come. In 1946 Chōkū compiled a tanka collection called *Mountain Top* containing poems by both father and son; in July 1949 he erected a memorial tablet for his son in a pine grove by the sea in Ichinomiya, Ishikawa Prefecture. Then, in 1953, father was buried in the same plot as son.

Reference to his son who will die in the war is frequently made in *Japanese Man*. Chōkū believed that of all young men his son was least equal to the challenge of war. As a result, Chōkū was guilt-ridden over his inability to provide a happy life for Harumi. The time would come when he would naturally cry out for the return of his son. About twelve hundred years previously Prince Arima was hanged for treason, as was one of his followers; namely, a man with the highly unusual name of Shioya-no-Murajiko-no-Shiro. The uniqueness of such a name never left Chōkū. He remembered it and at the same time he had been re-reading *Nihon Shoki* (The Chronicles of Japan). He was filled with the sense of sorrowful destiny. In May 1946 Chōkū organized a study-group, in his home, of *The Chronicles of Japan*, this in memory of Harumi. The group continued until his death.

The unusual name must have lain deeply buried in Chōkū's heart. There profound sorrows gathered and depressed him: the war's defeat, his son's death and the accumulated events of old age. His elegiac tanka over Harumi's death come like explosions against a wall. Unlike ordinary tanka, they are not indirect, and this is a rare approach to tanka in the case of Chōkū's. The depth of the grief would not be contained but must directly out. These tanka overflow with feelings.

IIDA DAKOTSU (1885-1962)

The Death of a Stern Father
(from *Images*)

"For the Soul of a man: Fortunate, Virtuous and Righteous"

Ah, my father,
dead in the darkness,
covered by frozen clouds!

Abandoned too soon
by mother and father,
I hear grass grumble underfoot.

Because his body has grown cold
the scent of medicine
sharpens the air.

His futon is still warm.
When I remove the foot-warmer
the water sloshes around.

Death most closely
approaches his face
by winter candlelight.

The pillow faces north
and summons
swirling coldness in the scented air.

A Purification Rite Performed in Darkness at the Crematory Grounds

By a mountain stream
a storm at night
passionately fans the bonfire.

The paper lantern I set down
away from the blaze
seems frozen to the bone.

Thin, thin the body,
when I lay a sword
across his shroud.

Candlelight feints
on the golden screen
turned upside down.

Funeral Rite

How quickly, so quickly
this winter day
the coffin departs....

And even as shadows descend
this winter's day
the funeral fire gives no smoke....

As we proceed with the urn
a myriad of woolly aphids
speckle the air.

In the winter of 1943 Dakotsu lost his father. The ancestors lived in a mountain village called Sakaigawa in the Yatsushiro district of Kōshū (now called Yamanashi Prefecture). This family of farmers were privileged from generation to generation to use the surname of Iida and bear the Iida sword. The subtitle "The Death of a Stern Father" is quite rhetorical but it permits us to imagine how an old rural family observed traditional funeral rites.

The image of a dead body radiating the scent of medicine brings the olfactory sense into sharp focus. The father's dead face seen "by winter candlelight" reveals that although his soul has departed it still hovers nearby. The placing of a sword across the shroud is a talismanic act. Dakotsu was moved to deeper pity by the collapsing of the shroud under the weight of the sword.

The burial rite was performed at night by lantern light, the coffin being carried to the field where the body would be cremated. Even at that time this sort of rite was rarely observed in Tokyo.

Oddly—at least at first blush—the coffin was carried from the house at a quite rapid pace (it was supposed to be so rapid as to render the coffin invisible).

However sonorous this series of haiku, the poet's stance is unflaggingly sincere and serious from start to finish.

GOTŌ MIYOKO (1898-1978)

An Empty Shell
(from *A Mother's Tanka*)

At the end of autumn
twigs and leaves,
wind-blown,
clatter
like bones.

Will the lost child
come fluttering
the sleeves of her kimono
by moonlight
and swing on the silvery swing?

Somehow less involved,
her father
will not quite think of her
as his own
flesh and blood.

The one
who gives life and soul
to her child
but cannot replace flesh and blood
is called 'mother'.

Young leaves,
windows, wet;
the air moist—
my young child's grave
must also be wet.

One night
her hair brushed against
a tree trunk.
I wonder, does the tree still
sigh in secret?

The light of the full moon
flows and dances.
My daughter
has become
a child of light.

She is gone.
Yet for a moment
she smiled in my heart.
Can it be that I shall once again
be happy?

Like spring,
she galloped away.
Her hair, her eyes.......
Wind-blown,
she vanished.

Time in my heart
blurred; stopped dead.
Nothing remains there
but my memory
of her.

No one is more inconsolable than a mother grieving over her daughter's death. The loss of one's own flesh and blood is a supreme loss.

These tanka are born out of the essence of motherhood. A father's sense of loss, she insists, is less profound. Sacrifice body and soul as she might, in the end such sacrifice was not enough. What it means to be a mother, after all, is to endure this karma, this grief, she supposed.

The daughter was in fact already a young adult. "She is gone" tells us that her daughter, in the mother's memory, appeared and smiled, and that that smile was engraved on her heart. Guilt-ridden over too little attention given, the mother is seized with grief whereas the daughter appears carefree. While asking "Can it be......that I shall...be happy?" Miyoko is actually weeping at heart. The very innocence of the daughter's smile intensifies her grief all the more.

ISHIDA HAKYŌ (1913-1967)

Life is Precious
(from *Life is Precious*)

At sunset
silver grass
and my mother at prayer....

Coxcombs in the garden
remind me of nothing but
a stretcher.

Into the chamber pot
....
the gurgling of a mountain spring.

When I dreamed
I passed over the peak—
was it dew or frost?

That I lived long enough
to see in Indian summer
these exquisite branches!

Sleepless, I waken and see
a pitcher of water
beginning to freeze.

Helped to a sitting position
all at once the onrush
of winter frost floods my eyes.

We see a corpse
carried off through the back gate
of the leafless garden.

(Written after my first post-operative outing)

I dragged my dangerously thin shadow
along the road
of leafless trees.

Where woolly aphids circle
is at the back gate
where corpses depart.

Patients warm
their pale slender fingers
over a pile of burning leaves.

In the dawn corridor,
dim by snow-light,
a stretcher waits.

In the holding room
a few people gather and stare.
Outside the snow is silent, thick, swift.

(My fellow-patient, Takeda, dies)

Like the plum blossoms,
properly arrayed on only one branch:
Mr. Takeda's attitude on the stretcher.

Wiping the sweat off with my hand
I heft the number of days
I have left.

Ill and despondent,
we lean over and stare at
the ant hole.

Hearing the wind-bell before dawn
click and twinkle,
goose bumps cover my misery.

In March 1944 Hakyō was drafted and sent to Wu-ti in China, and promptly came down with pleurisy. He was repatriated and discharged in 1945. Pleurisy struck him a second time in September 1947. He coughed up vast quantities of bloody phlegm and grew extremely weak. In May 1948 he was hospitalized in Kiyose Village, Tokyo, in the Tokyo Sanitorium where twice a year he had a thoracoplastic operation. A plastic ball was implanted in his lung cavity. In those days this operation was referred to as a "ping- pong ball." It was, in his case, of little use, for after all this operation was still in an experimental stage

The *Life is Precious* haiku are a sort of pre-and post-sanitorium diary. In the immediate post-war period, operations involving plastic implantations were indeed life-threatening. In haiku after haiku, on the verge of death, he gazed resolutely at hard reality.

In the fourth haiku he dreams he is climbing a mountain with great difficulty and is unaware whether he is awake or asleep. The "dew or frost" stands for the bitterness of hard reality

The fifth haiku exudes a brightness as though to relieve our heavy hearts, while in the sixth he watches water freeze in darkness—and our blood runs cold.

In the tenth haiku the gate referred to is the sanitorium's so-called" Unclean Gate" through which corpses were removed. (Of course the front gate was not used for this purpose.) The morgue was probably a quiet, isolated small cabin behind the sanitorium which at that time was, as Hakyō could see from his window, shrouded in snow.

Although he himself narrowly escaped death, he frequently had to watch his friends of the day before being carried away. For this reason he was highly conscious in each moment of the time remaining to him. Tortured by the dark thoughts that rose out of the very center of his being, he lay awake even at midnight.

MIYOSHI TATSUJI

Losing My Friend
(from *A Southern Exposure*)

Departure

At midnight a plane came out of a hangar,
coughed four times
and spit up a bloody rose:

Mr. Kajii, you soared up to heaven.
My friend, wait a little. I'll join you in a moment.

Mourning Clothes

At high noon in spring a passing crow calls.
My heart wears black … Ah, friend—I lean against the window.

Friend! The crow's call vanishes. Girls walk among the trees.
I behold for a mere moment life shining in their beautiful black hair.

These two poems were written in memory of Kajii Motojirō who had been
Tatsuji's friend since Dai-san High School (now Kyoto University) days. The
two men had regularly contributed to the literary magazine *Blue Sky*. Kajii died
on 24th March 1932.

He died from tuberculosis, which Tatuji also suffered from, complicated in
his case by excessive worry about his heart. He was hospitalized in an
institution affiliated with Tokyo Women's Medical School. Thus in the poem
"Departure" he hints at his own death: "I'll join you in a moment."

ITŌ SHIZUO (1906-1953)

Naturally, Quite Naturally
(from *Summer Flowers*)

A child found a bird struggling in a bush
and didn't let it go.
Badly wounded,
it pecked at his finger violently.

The boy's caress thus rejected,
he flung it away as hard as he could,
but the bird, oddly, kicked at the air,
flipped over and naturally lighted on a small branch.

Naturally? Yes, quite naturally!
But then all at once the boy saw it
fall to earth like a stone—
there it lay on its back, still....

The bird dies in a moment of high excitation. The alert boy plucks this wounded
bird from the bush, his intentions, far from evil, are wholly benevolent. The
bird of course senses no caress. The bird struggles violently to escape and pecks
his finger; whereas the boy, feeling betrayed, flings it away in wonder and
anger. Fortunately the bird recovers its wings in mid-air and grasps a tree
branch.

Time stopped in the moment of its alighting: "Naturally? Yes, quite naturally!" Yet almost at once time began to move again, for the bird fell to earth and there, easily, "it lay on its back, still...." It died simply as though in an uneventful natural death. The poem, because it is an artful model, thus depicts a fictive incident. The fright, the horror, the psychological conflict of the actual incident, ending in death, are utterly hidden from view.

Which is betrayed—boy or bird? What is illustrated is the ease with which a caress can turn into an act of brutality. The most beautiful thing is the bird pecking desperately at his finger, expressing its vital life force and thereby dying. The imagined natural death is a revelation of this vital life force. Even though there was no battle at all between the boy and the bird but only an intended caress that turned at once into a violent counter-intention, the bird lay dead on its back.

KUSANO SHIMPEI (1903-1988)

The Death of Grima
(from *The Hundredth Class*)

Grima died when the boy who caught it threw it down
Rurida, bereft,
picked a violet
and put it in Grima's mouth.

She grieved beside him for half-a-day and returned to the water.
The tempting croaking of her fellows penetrated her guts.
She choked on a fountain of tears.

Both Grima and the violet
withered
in the sunlight.

Shimpei wrote many frog poems, all of them showing as much affection for such small creatures as for people. No. To be more exact, he finds human nature in frogs; that is, good and evil, or innocence.

The dead frog's mouth holding Rurida's violet now looks like a vase. Grima's death is tragically imposed from without in an unresisting, passive world. It results from the whimsical yet cruel self-entertainment of a boy. Grima's death and Rurida's grief are a result of what is for him merely a sort of practical joke.

A pleasure-seeking chorus of frogs calls everywhere around them as though Grima's death and Rurida's grief were unknown to them. Beginning to feel suffocated, Rurida enters the water with tearful eyes. The strong summer sun does its work on a shrivelling Grima. For nature and for community, death is merely death—nothing more.

Albeit a brief little poem, strong feelings are roused.

MURANO SHIRŌ (1901-1975)

Deer
(from *The Journal of a Stray Sheep*)

A deer stood still in the setting sun
at the edge of the woods.
He knew that his small forehead
was being aimed at.
But how could he avoid it?
He kept still,
looking toward the village.
The moment left to him
glittered like gold
against the vast darkness
of the deep woods.

A deer clearly senses that a hunter has drawn a bead on him and that death is certain. He cannot escape or deny it. Fate will be fulfilled in the next moment. In his last moment his life will shine and thus he stands in the rapture of this final and intense shining. The blackness of the woods looms behind him, the distant village ahead. The threshold between the dark woods and the still sunlit village is created and in it the handsome figure stands, as slender as a lily—stands for the eternity of a moment.

INOUE YASUSHI (1897-1991)

Friend
(from *The North Country*)

Why didn't I ever think of
anything as obvious?
You could have found no other way
to come back to your defeated country
than by dragging along the floor of the straits.

Yasushi thinks of his friend who was killed in the war and grieves over that
irreplaceable loss. In ruminating he imagines his friend's return, not as ashes;
but plodding along "the valley of the shadow of death" on the bottom of the
straits. He has no other choice. Having hit upon this idea, Yasushi is plunged
in grief.

NAKAHARA CHŪYA

Bones
(from *Songs of Bygone Days*)

Look at these! It's my bones!
Made of the misery I had while I lived,
free of the wretched flesh
and washed indifferently by rain.
The ends of the bones protrude.

They are lustreless.
To no point at all
they absorb the rain.
Wind-blown,
they reflect a shard of the sky.

When I was alive
these bones would sit among customers
in a cheap restaurant,

and now it's funny to think of their eating
boiled greens with soy sauce.

Look at these! They're my bones—
is it I looking at them? That's funny.
The left-over soul
visits the bones again
and—what?—looks them over?

Is it I? Standing
on the dying grass by the brook
in my hometown—is it I?
They're about as tall as a sign board
and, at their ends, indifferently sharp.

Chūya wrote this poem in 1934 at the age of twenty-six. We may feel inclined to laugh at him, a young inexperienced fellow writing such a poem as this. Yet considering that he died in 1937, only a few years were left to him.

His antic tone is characteristic, though we all the more feel a lump in our throat when such a subject is put in this way. In its expression the poem ultimately takes on a tentative, self-conscious aspect. The theme of the poem—"looking beyond the grave"—is inseparable from the tone.

Seen from the perspective of our death, all our life-long troubles come to seem ludicrous. How preposterous to have eaten boiled greens sprinkled with soy sauce in a greasy spoon! The more he says it is "funny," the deeper the poem sinks into the depths of sadness. The antic feel and movement of the poem somehow strike at the truth of life as it is.

III

Human Existence

NATSUME SŌSEKI (1867-1916)

September 15
(from his journal)

Autumn shakes the mountain trees bare.
I close the door and lie at ease on the tatami,
kept company by my cold shadow.
A single boat in the shoals.....fine rain on the lotus flowers.
Steeped in loneliness, the night deep and dark, I burn incense—
scent and candlelight enhance the characters.
Gazing beyond the rain and clouds,
I listen to the bell sifting through the trees.

In the process of writing his novel *Light and Darkness*, which was being serialized in a newspaper, Sōseki was in the habit of writing installments in the morning and in the afternoon a form of Chinese verse called *lüshi* consisting of eight lines of seven characters each. In letters to Akutagawa Ryūnosuke (1892-1927) and Kume Masao (1891-1952), Sōseki states: "When writing a novel I feel immersed in the hectic routines of the real world, and so I determined to escape the hustle and bustle by writing a Chinese poem." In 1916, between the night of August 14 and the night of November 20, he composed seventy-odd *lüshi*.

In the original, ll. 3-4 and 5-6 comprise couplets. The *lüshi*—in Japanese "*risshi*"—is severely demanding technically and requires objective observations about the natural world. Subjective lyricism is prohibited. Contrary to fact, Sōseki places himself in a humble thatched cottage overlooking a river. The poem affords an escape from the "real" world. The deep desolation of the loneliness that engulfed him in his last years comes out very clearly. In my opinion the highest poetic peak in the general age of which Sōseki was a part is reached in his Chinese poems.

HORIGUCHI DAIGAKU

A Muddy Mouse
(from *A New Path*)

A muddy mouse lives all day
in a muddy paddy.
Ah, he says, mud-spattered,
life is tedious.

Oh Sun! Master Sun!
No matter how often I call,
the peach-colored sun doesn't answer.
The operator, oh, is deaf and unkind
and doesn't answer.

Life is filled with crossed wires
and busy signals.

The moon appears from behind the mountain
and the world becomes a silver night.
A muddy mouse falls asleep in a muddy paddy,
embracing a female mouse.

When I was young I memorized a dozen such poems by Daigaku and some of them still come easily to mind. They are colloquial and rhythmically buoyant. This particular poem is composed of mostly seven- and five-syllable lines.

For this reason and for its wit or humor, and at the same time because the melancholy of an empty life is revealed, the poem suited my taste. Stanzas one and four are in seven- and five-syllable lines, respectively. It is interesting to note that the two middle stanzas depart from the regularity of both rhythm and content shown in stanzas one and four. In my youth I found great pleasure in rolling his phrases off the tip of my tongue. It was titillating to suck the poem's bones dry of their youthful vitality.

SAIJŌ YASO (1892-1970)

Giving My Dog Away
(from *Unpublished Poems*)

I gave my dog away,
the loving dog I had for six years.
It had a violent temper and would bite at random.
All the neighbors complained.

He got in a black car and crouched in a corner,
and left for a farmhouse in Chiba
where he could howl at the night moon
and protect otters from thieves.

I'm not a bit lonely.
Some day I'll bid the earth farewell
with its pleasant wind, its light
and gentle eyes and voices.

To my ever malleable, sentimental heart
I took a whip
and blew a whistle,
and sent the dog away.

This poem is stylistically far removed from the symbolistic elegance of *Gold Dust*, his first collection. His thoughts about loneliness and his sense of desolation seem to have sunk to the very bottom of his soul. The blunt expression, "I gave my dog away", mirrors the state of his soul as he parts from his lonely life's single faithful companion. His sorrowful voice is heard straining here as he speaks from the depth of his soul in the face of his impending death. "I gave my dog away" is a mere bluff. The last lingering image is that of his loneliness in the absence of his dog: [I] "sent the dog away."

KANEKO MITSUHARU (1895-1975)

Wash Basin
(from *Elegies for Women*)

(I had always thought that a wash basin was only used for washing hands and face, but the Javanese fill it with curry soup boiled with mutton, fish, chicken and fruit, and wait for customers in the shade of the blossoming silk tree; while women in Canton straddle it and openly urinate in front of prospective 'customers', thus making the lonely sound of urine being expelled.)

A lonely sound
in a wash basin.

Boats anchored in the rain
in a cape at twilight.

Endless echoes
sway
and swerve
in my weary heart.

As long as we live
you must listen, ears,

To the lonely sounds
in a wash basin.

Mitsuharu reached Singapore at last in November 1931 on his return from his second trip to Europe. He wrote this poem while in the Malay Peninsula. Although he had not written poems for a long time, he was softened and his poetic bent was restored by primitive nature and the simple life in Southeast Asia.

In "A lonely sound/in a wash basin" he perceived the lonely sound of our life universally. That is all the poem is about and the deep meaning—no, the deep meaninglessness or nothingness of this life reverberates in each word. However brief this poem, it is surprisingly full of overtones.

IBUSE MASUJI (1898-1993)

A Drinking Song
(A translation from the Chinese of Yu Wu-ling, from Ibuse's *Poems of Exorcism*)

Please take this cup
and let me fill it with wine
Wind scatters the petals.
Life is saying good-bye.

In *Poems of Exorcism* some dozen Chinese poems are given in translation. All of them are done—unlike the fixed Chinese form—in the colloquial language of Ibuse's free verse. The last line distinguishes Ibuse as the best of the translators from the Chinese. Sorrow, as seen in this poem, is an aspect of life itself. Thus, one reasons, "Let's drink this night to our hearts' content." This poem is virtually Ibuse's rather than the Chinese poet's, for it is so "creative" that it is Ibuse of whom we are conscious.

INOUE YASUSHI

Yuan Shih
(from *The North Country*)

In southwestern Hêpei Province in the village
of Yuan Shih we busily piled up sandbags atop
a crumbling castle wall. Each of us was
engaged in reinforcing the fort before sunset
and before the enemy came. The advent of a
strangely quiet hush at that time, the thickets
beyond the peaceful villages in early winter,
a great flock of birds headed south beyond
the horizon, smoke signals risen from the
foothills of a distant mountain in the west,
and casual conversations we three had at that
time—only I, I alone, recall these matters.
The following day the two friends I stood between
were no longer in this world.
Whatever happened that night? Though there
was no fiercely sustained battle, something cold

that ineluctably revealed the march of fate
filled the darkness. We were not conscious
of a victory. The silent rain fell steadily
like sulfuric acid on our hearts.

Inoue here records the front line of battle. Two friends were killed. The words are rather matter of fact, except for Inoue's use of "something cold" in the darkness, which alludes to the inevitability of things. Here is a lonely soul who has tasted war to the full.

OGATA KAMENOSUKE (1900-1942)

The Old Man Next Door is at Death's Door
(from *The Street of Stained Glass*)

The old man next door is at death's door.

For some reason
I can't help but worry about him.
I hear his feeble footsteps.
He quietly opens the door and goes in
and everything is silent.

Strangely, I've seen him quite often
and it seems as if
he's about to enter my place by mistake.

Is he referring to his apartment's neighbor? Kamenosuke seems to believe the old fellow is close to death and so he worries about him. Anxiety sustained at length is debilitating, the more so when no sound is heard inside the old man's apartment. The poet appears to fear, when he thinks the old man might mistakenly enter his apartment, that "Death" himself might be coming in.

KUSANO SHIMPEI

Conversation on an Autumn Night
(from *The Hundredth Class*)

Cold, isn't it?
Yeah, it's cold.
The crickets sure are loud.
Uh. Sure are.
Almost time to go to sleep.
Uh, I hate sleeping in the dirt.
You've lost weight, haven't you?
Gee, so've you—a lot!
Where does this pain of mine come from?
Probably your stomach's bad, huh?
Remove my stomach and I'm probably done for.
Huh! I don't wanna die.
Cold, isn't it?
The crickets sure are loud.

Two frogs are conversing. The autumn night is cold. They will soon hollow out holes to sleep in and before very long they will hibernate for the winter. They suffer from hunger pangs, which is where the "stomach" comes in—not the heart. "I don't wanna die." indicates that their hunger is intense, their spirits depressed.

Frozen in body and soul, shivering, these two frogs speaking in a desolate field suggest the absolute loneliness of human existence. In reading this poem we ourselves shiver badly.

MARUYAMA KAORU (1899-1974)

Along the Way
(from *Inside a Flower*)

Darkness is falling.
Snowflakes glitter—
an uncanny light, like twilight.

My eyes are steeped in light.
The snow disappears;
the whole landscape vanishes.
I blindly feel my way in the pearly light. ·

Where am I going, I wonder?
There's no snow beneath me.
I'm walking toward the north of my life.

Here midway in my life,
I cough coldly once...twice....

Kaoru evacuated the city for a mountain village in Yamagata Prefecture. The war was raging. Teaching there in a school, he wrote a series of poems called "A Dream of the North", of which this is one. In the title poem of that series he states that, "Living in the north,/Living in the snow,/I began to think even more of snow and ice./Sitting alone,/I began to turn toward desolation." These lines will stand in explication of "Along the Way". When he reached middle-age he seemed to turn from the warmth of his hometown on the south coast to the bleakness of the north. His mood, obviously, is that of a soul prepared to steep itself in frigid Stoicism.

He walks north in a snow storm, in his imagination—"I blindly feel my way in the pearly light."—this light being the color of light he has arrived at, finally, on the brink of hopelessness. He is unaware of a destination; only the direction "north" turns in his mind. For the lonely, life is a sad and solitary journey. The last two lines restore us to our senses. The true spirit of Stoicism felt here by Kaoru is preserved, even in his desolation, by a bit of humor.

IV

Songs of Daily Life

TAKAMURA KŌTARŌ

Supper at Yonekyū

Oppressively sultry, this August night at Yonekyū Restaurant.

Two large tatami rooms separated by open shoji doors....
a sea of humanity riveted to the mats....
a cloud of Bat cigarette smoke; voices rise and strike like lightning....
To my left and right, before, behind,
faces, hats, headbands, men half-nude, uproarious din,
beer bottles, sake, chopsticks, glasses, sake cups,
bubbling sukiyaki pots, bland Chinese rice....
A few crude Amazons coiffured like butterflies
bustle about, keeping the hot storm under control;
dolls, they seem worked by a string,
fetching things they read in the palms of their hands.

Oppressively sultry, this August night at Yonekyū Restaurant.

None too soon a soft breeze from the southern azure sky
where the Scorpion lives dispels the stench of onion and tobacco smoke;
is fanned about by all the diners.
I thoroughly enjoy my post-prandial green tea.
My friend, as usual, lights his fine Asahi cigarette.
After eating and drinking we fall quiet.
On the ocean's floor a rumbling,
and a symphony of vision and reality is whispered.
Hi, Pop! Been a long time. Sit over here.
Say, Okin-san, that fellow's bill is under the clock!
So, old fellow, our platoon at the bridge....
Hey, where's our sake? Where? Huh?
Aw, don't be so stuck-up!
I mean, how innocent can you get!
See that girl? She's a Socialist. Terribly quiet, isn't she?
By the way, Boss, why don't you fix my...?
I know, I know. I'll do it. Just hold your horses....

What's closing time here?
11:30. No need to hurry.
How can you sweat so much and stay so busy?
Check?   What, an egg and a beer? 1.35 yen....
Whoops! Here's another bottle hiding away! That'll make it 1.80....
Oh, sorry.... Who do you want?.....

Oppressively sultry, this August night at Yonekyū Restaurant.

Sitting by their many hibachis
some guests build the world's most cozy nest
and enjoy the great pleasure of their appetite.
Just as in the public bath where they wash their souls,
here they also strive to relax, open up, enjoy,
expelling all their inner darkness,
and drink, eat, shout, laugh and even at times yell.
Revelling in the revealed shades of human affections,
tonight, at least, they drink in fine fettle.
Though tomorrow they return to their coal-black work,
tonight they freely lavish money on the elderly and young wives.
The tattooed punks shrink before the scolding Amazons.
To keep their new clothes clean, they stir the sukiyaki carefully.
Some specially enjoy the food because they earned it themselves.
A crowd, a crowd, a crowd.

Oppressively sultry, this August night at Yonekyū Restaurant.

My friend and I are almost beside ourselves with joy
over Yonekyū's heaping panful of delicious beef.
In the gluttony and din of this crowd
we find something of our true animal nature;
we also find wonder in that Mother Nature has so capriciously blessed man.
I am moved to tears by the bits and pieces of sentimental stories I overhear.
We express great love to the old head waitress who bids us goodbye.
As one guest, anyway, I do my best to shower sincere gratitude on her
and leave remarkably refreshed and feeling really vigorous.

Oppressively sultry, this August night at Yonekyū Restaurant.

This poem "takes place" at the height of the summer at a very popular sukiyaki restaurant. It was formerly located at Senzoku-chō in Asakusa, Tokyo. A lot of people are ravenously hungry as the sukiyaki cooks in its pans. The sturdy women scurry up and down the narrow aisles between the tables in these tatami rooms. People of every station are among the "faces, hats, headbands, men half-nude, uproarious din...."

His dinner over, his friend beside him, Kōtarō sips his comforting green tea while looking around and overhearing various conversations in which fragments of daily life are scattered about. This is a favorite retreat of common people, a pleasure resort for dining and talking—"a public bath of the spirit" to heal their fragmented minds and hearts. A waitress's father is among the guests and so are a soldier and his uncle, an arrogant man, a woman Socialist, a carpenter, a frugal married couple, a craftsman spending his entire day's wage oblivious to tomorrow, and a tattooed man cowed by a waitress's scolding.

Kōtarō is full of praise for the heap of beef before him and for the glad animality of the people, and then listens to the heart-warming stories people are telling. Finally he applauds the head waitress for her aplomb. He has caught a glimpse of the joys and the stories of some of Tokyo's lower class people. His sympathy for them is deep for he himself was born the son of a craftsman in a lower class area.

IBUSE MASUJI

A Lost Title
(from *Poems of Exorcism*)

Tonight a harvest moon—
and a time for missing our first love.
But forgetting everything,
we drink alone tonight at Yoshinoya.

Say, Haru, how about some chopped octopus?
With salt, please.
And make sure the sake's hot.
And a dish of green soybeans.

Ha! The octopus looks like a belly button.
So, we sit down and sit tall
and quietly pour the sake.
The soybeans breathe steam.

Tonight a harvest moon—
and a time for missing our first love.
But forgetting everything,
we drink alone tonight at Yoshinoya.

Many men of letters frequented Yoshinoya, which sat beside a small waterway in Shimbashi. In pre-war days I used to go there with Kawakami Tetsutarō and Yoshida Ken'ichi, literary critics. After every meeting of our literary club "Critique", we regularly stopped in at Yoshinoya for a bowl of rice and raw tuna as our final dish.

The owner's nickname was Haru. "But forgetting everything" introduces a note of humor and by "we drink alone" he suggests that each man is alone with his sake-lover. In Japanese culture the harvest moon and green soybeans are inevitably associated; however, cherishing one's first love under a harvest moon in particular is quite strange. Oblivious to everything, he drinks alone in this his last stop while bar-hopping. The chopped octopii that resemble belly buttons, his sitting down properly in his chair and concentrating all his energy in his abdomen, and his feeling refreshed and pouring his sake quietly all give an accurate glimpse of the true lover of sake.

Ibuse creates a fine poetic feeling in creating this droll atmosphere.

KIYAMA SHŌHEI (1904-68)

Smacking One's Lips Over Rice
(from *The Poems of Kiyama Shōhei*)

Guys eating supper at the counter
sound like cats
lapping up water.

Ah, twilight loneliness.
The men are licking their fifteen sen-platters clean.

In pre-war days lunch at a lunch counter used to cost fifteen sen. At supper time the blue collar men jamming the cafés slurped lustily. Kiyama, sitting among them, hears their noisy eating and mutters to himself. Their lips macking in its solitariness makes the poet aware of his loneliness. The sound is one that should be contained; one that mothers tell their children not to make. He finds himself eating among those slurping noises and feels lonely. The plain sounds of men eating make us feel the radical loneliness of human existence.

KAWAKAMI HAJIME (1879-1946)

Miso
(from *Traveller*)

I went around to Kantsune's for New Year's miso
as a special treat.
The owner's wife looked at me,
checked to see if my name was on the list
and whispered something to her husband; then said,
'Is your wife still away?
Inconvenient, isn't it?'
Her words were quite thoughtful.
She did not let the lined-up guests see
that she gave me a double allowance of miso,
and deliberately kept silent about it.
I'm unusually fond of miso.
I took my wooden pail
and left the store with a fine feeling.
I went on my way to a favorite flower shop
and with thirty sen
bought a white chrysanthemum.
The sky was cold and cloudy.
I scrunched up my shoulders and walked briskly
down Yoshida Ōji Avenue.
I was on my way home
in the gathering dusk.
The taro that I had left boiling
on the hibachi by the writing desk
was soft, ready to eat.
They were reddish ones from the garden
of my house in my hometown.
They were large but they were done.
I mixed a little sugar into the white miso
and spread it on a taro,
boiled and ate it.

Ah, those mushy taro,
steaming hot!
No need to add any spices.
I told myself, 'Oh, are these good!'
After eating supper
I recalled the years of my abject poverty
and thought about the left-over future.
I felt rich
and naturally self-contented.

(1944, New Year's Day)

Here rationing during the war years is recalled. In his wife's absence Kawakami goes to purchase his own miso [fermented soybean paste]. 1943 was drawing to a close. The woman's kindness to him at the sake store filled him with delight—extraordinary delight.

His desertion of the Communist movement somewhat earlier had resulted as well in a separation from his own true feelings and identity; however, even in this state of mind he was able to appreciate deeply the gift so freely given. The experience rather sustained him at this point in his life. He was conscious, too, of the receipt of taro from his hometown.

Not a professional poet, and in fact naïve, he writes a poem which carries no ornamentation in its expression of gratitude to others; *joie de vivre* is felt, also, in his humble life.

NAKAGAWA KAZUMASA (1893-1991)

An Impoverished Mother
(from *Strangers*)

People are all sad.
It isn't only my mother
who came along the road late at night
carrying a small bag of rice.

Tonight
I saw a poor woman returning with
a small slice of salted salmon.
She has no choice in this life

but to get her salmon
and carry her baby on her back.
Little child, you who are so innocent,
warm on your mother's back,
what she'll give you is delicious.

Sleep, lovely child,
in contentment.
Sleep, lovely child.
When you were really little
your mother was even poorer
and struggled to raise and protect you.

People are all struggling to live.
And all are sad.
Yet this mother protects her child.
And though she buys her thin slice of salmon
wrapped in newspaper,
she nonetheless has the strength
to carry on
the business of life and living.

Cherish your child!
A mother bearing her child on her back
is pitiable
and heartrending.

Kazumasa was well-known as a painter. This poem is tinged with something like Mushanokōji Saneatsu's humanism but, unlike Mushanokōji's work, also contains a stark sense of real life.

Buying 1.8 liters of rice indicates impoverishment. Although he must have known that "isshō-gai" (1.8 liters) represented great poverty, he had no knowledge that "her thin slice of salmon" represented even greater poverty. The piece of salmon must have been very thin indeed. It goes almost without saying that the mother let the child eat as much as possible while she made herself content with a morsel.

Great poverty or not, people will raise their children. The mother will provide under the necessity to protect her child. That parents will do so is, the poet feels, one of this life's fortunate occurrences, even if parents are in the depths of despair. The sadness of all of life is epitomized by the mother carrying "her baby on her back."

SENGE MOTOMARO (1888-1948)

A Mother and Two Children
(from *I Saw*)

In front of the quiet little rice cake shop
on the outskirts of town, late on New Year's eve,
two children were begging their mother to buy some.
She wanted to,
and through the window saw some cakes remaining.
The card priced them at thirteen sen.
She stood there for quite a long time;
her children on either side, hanging on her sleeves,
peered through the glass and saw the card by the light of an oil lamp.
She pulled her wallet out from her sash
and counted her money in the dim light.
The three all wondered whether they could buy some
and stood quietly, riveted to the spot.
Silence looked on in agony and anxiety.
The moon peeked through a still, white cloud
and looked hard at them, wondering what would happen.
Ten minutes passed!
She sighed inaudibly and began to walk away from the cold town.
The children obediently followed,
knowing that the rice cakes were beyond their reach.
The air seemed to breathe a sigh of relief at last.
Moon and cloud began moving.
Everything shifted and passed in the deserted town.
No one saw anything.
The town sank into eternal silence;
only a god saw.
Walking away, the three might have been
a woman and her children, god-sent,
a noble, tender, beautiful mother and two gentle angels
or a poor mother and her children through the late night on New Year's eve
intending to buy rice cakes after the town slept.

Motomaro belonged to the White Birch group of poets, as did Nakagawa Kazumasa. Although they had something in common, Nakagawa's language was literary while Senge's was completely colloquial and garrulous.

New Year's eve, a poor mother with her two children standing longingly, hesitantly, in front of the rice cake store—the climax comes when Silence in agony and with baited breath freezes time. The moment passes. As they begin resignedly walking away, we can at last breathe easily. Although the three will greet New Year's day without rice cakes, the poet no longer cares about that. Although he naturally sees here what nobody else sees, he seems to have disappeared. But a god may have looked on, too; or they might by chance have been a woman and two children sent by a god. His gift of gab serves him in the first part of the poem and yet he does not end the poem in a deft and definitive manner.

NAKA KANSUKE (1885-1955)

Salted Salmon
(from *Asuka*)

Ah, I'm rich tonight!
I have a whole half-glass of sake.
Salted salmon smells extravagant on the plate.
I am sated with steaming rice and barley.
I recall abandoning
my family,
the world,
people,
parents and relatives;
suffering from my own wrath,
fury,
doubt,
despair,
and illness gnawing at my heart and bones;
lingering on the verge of death,
catching my breath without respite.
I recall
madly craving a piece of salted salmon
in a fish shop on the outskirts of town
where I had gone to get some medicine.

Look at this beautiful red coral!
A piece of oily, sweet-salted salmon
makes me think of the old days.
My eyes glaze over and I drop my chopsticks.

"Salted salmon" was a thing deeply embedded in the mind of Tokyoites. Kansuke is able to claim, "Ah, I'm rich tonight!" by a mere reference to salted salmon, a half-glass of sake and hot rice and barley. Having abandoned his home and family, and sick almost unto death, he deeply hungered for a slice of salted salmon—recalling his circumstances, the poet grows very nostalgic.

The description asks no additions. It is perfectly simple. It pays homage to salted salmon. "Look at this beautiful red coral!/A piece of oily, sweet-salted salmon."—here is the real heart of the poem and it will be at once perfectly satisfying to any lover of salted salmon. The words bring the object—and its veritable taste!—to life. We are convinced that the poet seriously considers himself rich.

MUSHANOKŌJI SANEATSU (1885-1976)

Live to the End of the World!
(from *The Poems of Mushanokōji Saneatsu*)

Live, live, live to the end of the world!
Even if you die, live!
Live in the light that shines from and to eternity.
Live in the river of life!
My law orders you to live.
I respect those who obey me and work.
In their work I hear the words of the king of Life.
As long as we live, we live,
and listen to the king's order,
and hear the sound of the flowing river of Life.
Listen! Won't you?
Live, live, live to the end of the world!
Even if you die, live along the living road!
Live
and pass the baton of life along!
Listen to the king taking long strides,
swaggering.
Listen, listen, listen to the footsteps of Life!

The poem above is an instance of Saneatsu's artless yet endearing poetry. Although one might object to calling it a poem at all, the fact is that it demonstrates a poetic mind more than most of the poetry of its time. We find in it no concrete objects such as are found in the work of Senge Motomaro and Nakagawa Kazumasa. Saneatsu's poetic mind is more vivid than theirs.

He listens in his heart to "the words of the king of Life." These words bid him to keep on working. No, he may be listening in his work to the rhythms of "the sound of the flowing river of Life." Either way would suffice. The point is to keep on living, hearing in life "the footsteps of Life."

No poet before had expressed himself so directly, frankly, simply and boldly. He expresses his thoughts in words that occur in the actual conscious moments of ordinary life.

ISHIKAWA TAKUBOKU

Songs of Self-Love
(from *A Handful of Sand*)

I am prepared
to die
searching for
the pleasantest career
for myself.

Swaying along
with the crowd
in the Asakusa night,
I slip away
with a lonely heart.

Having reached
the very pinnacle,
I descended,
waving my hat
in spite of myself.

I once slipped into
an abandoned hut
and smoked a cigarette

just because—poor fellow!—
I wanted to be alone.

I wish I could
end my life
with a heart
like one leaping
from a higher place.

These days
there's something
I regret,
which is why I laugh
in my sleep.

Because as I walk home
my leaden heart
weighs me down,
I feel myself
getting stronger.

The smell of new ink….
When I
uncork the bottle
the smell is absorbed
by my empty stomach.

For me
sadness is being
snug in my futon
in the cold night,
enduring my thirst and hunger.

Slave as I might,
my life is
not easy.
I just look down at
my two hands.

I feel as if I can see
everything to come,

though
I cannot get rid of
this sadness.

One morning
as I was dreaming
a sad dream
I woke to the smell
of miso soup.

I don't know why
the tops
of the cliffs
in my head
tumble down day after day.

What does it feel like
to grow aware of who I am?
Sometimes, as I look absent-mindedly
at the walls of my room,
I am taken aback.

It is because I lack money
that all these thoughts
fill my head.

The autumn wind
blows.

In April 1907 Takuboku left Hokkaido, placed his family in the care of
Miyazaki Ikuu in Hakodate, and went alone to Tokyo, thus putting an end to his
vagrant life. Filled with passion for the new trend of naturalism in literature, he
determined with all his energy to write a novel; at this time, therefore, he in fact
abandoned his poetry and tanka.

Even in Tokyo, however, he did not gain a reputation in the literary and
journalistic world. On the other hand, tanka meetings were held monthly at the
Asanos' residence in Sendagaya and at the Ōgai house—Tidal Watchtower—in
the Sendagi section of Tokyo's Komagome district. There Takuboku was
required to write tanka. A reluctantly passionate spirit, he wrote some waggish
tanka, which, he said, were rather worthless. An unexpected result of his

mock-heroic work was that he freed himself from the technical, decorative rhetorical style of the New Poetry School. Albeit doggerel, his tanka were yet permeated with the truth of life's loneliness. An element of his nomadic life surfaced in his work.

In spite of his disclaimer about poetry and tanka, he was a born tanka poet and a true poet at heart. He could not quit. Tanka and poetry called upon him regularly. On the night of 23rd June 1908 he suddenly begin to write tanka while lying on his futon, and continued enthusiastically the whole night through. Just after dawn he took a stroll through the cemetery of a nearby temple; feeling refreshed, he ended up composing no less than 120 tanka. He worked unflaggingly until 11:00 a.m. A diary entry states that "My head has been brimful of tanka. Whatever I see or hear reduces to tanka." This had been for him an extraordinary experience. In fact by 2:00 a.m. of the next morning his output swelled to 141 tanka.

Until then he had concentrated on writing novels, suppressing his urge to write tanka, and thus the dam was ready to burst. Some of them, certainly, tended towards the rhetorical as seen in the work of the Morning Star tanka poets, but we can clearly see in the following tanka that he had taken a tremendous step towards becoming the unique Takuboku that we know:

(from *A Handful of Sand*)

Crouching on the white sand
of a small island
in this eastern sea,
I spill my tears,
playing with a tiny sand crab.

Tears
streaming down my face
I'll never forget
squeezing
a handful of sand.

Just for fun
I picked my mother up,
but her lightness so surprised me
I couldn't even take three steps.
I could only cry.

In the essay "Poems to Eat" Takuboku writes, "Just like a husband who has no justifiable reason to scold his child severely, I found some consolation in abusing the tanka form." In the long run he was unable to disengage himself from tanka and—let me put it this way—tanka went too far in its relations with him.

The tanka given above represent a fresh start for Takuboku; they are in the colloquial style and treat ordinary life. They are taken from the "Songs of Self-Love" section in *A Handful of Sand*. The "Songs of Self-Love" are a sort of minute-by-minute record of his life. In an essay entitled "Conversation between an Egotist and His Friend", he states "I compose tanka because I love life. I write them because I love myself."

V

Society and Human Beings

ISHIKAWA TAKUBOKU

After an Endless Argument
(from *A Steel Whistle and Whistling*)

We read quite a lot and dispute what we read,
our fiery eyes flashing like the eyes of the youth in 'Russia'
fifty years ago.
We discuss a plan of action
but no one pounds the table with his fist
and shouts 'V Narod!'

We know as a rule what we want
and what people want,
so we know what we ought to do.
We know better than the Russians did fifty years ago
but no one pounds the table with his fist
and shouts 'V Narod!'

We're young and we're together,
always ready to make things new.
We know that the old will die and we will win in the end.
Listen to our burning words, look at our burning eyes!
But no one pounds the table with his fist
and shouts 'V Narod!'

Ah, the third candle is lighted!
Gnats are floating in our teacups.
One young woman is as passionate as ever
but her eyes are glazed with weariness after an endless argument;
but no one pounds the table with his fist
and shouts 'V Narod!'

June 15, 1911—Tokyo

This is the first of a series of poems called *A Steel Whistle and Whistling* written in June 1911 and based on the ideology of anarchy with which Takuboku and his cohorts were increasingly sympathetic, after the so-called 1910 High Treason Incident (an anarchist plot to assasinate Emperor Meiji that led to the mass arrest of left wing activists and the execution of twelve of them). The poems in this series, although literary, are free, eloquent, grand and straight to the point.

"V Narod!" was a rallying cry among some student intelligentsia (for "narodniki") who believed in the principle of "agriculture first" (physiocracy). "Narodniki" in this context means "solidarity with the masses." The poem reflects some irritation with the Japanese intelligentsia who at this time were contemplative only, rather than doers (this of course included Takuboku himself).

Such young friends as Maruya Kiichi and Namiki Hisui often passionately discussed socialism with Takuboku. True, the poem doesn't deal directly with socialism, but the atmosphere of the poem seems somehow influenced by Takuboku's reading of the anarchist Kropotkin and others.

After an Endless Argument
(from *A Steel Whistle and Whistling*)

I understand the sadness
in a terrorist's heart—
the only heart in which
words and deeds are inseparable;
the heart that speaks with deeds
instead of stolen words;
the heart that will sacrifice itself and its body to the enemy.
So the sad heart is always only for the serious and earnest man.
After an endless argument,
sipping a spoon of cold cocoa,
the faint bitterness on my tongue
teaches me the sadness
in a terrorist's heart.

This is the second section of "After An Endless Argument," composed on the same day as the first poem in the section. Takuboku was introduced to terrorist ideas by Kanno Suga, the only female conspirator among the others, also executed on account of the 1910 High Treason Incident. Terrorist ideas were after all ineffective and not in keeping with the ideas Takuboku had gotten, especially from Kropotkin's writings. At the same time he could not help but feel deep sympathy with "the sadness/in a terrorist's heart." He wrote:

> Day by day
> the sadness in a terrorist's heart,
> which I thought far off
> is coming
> closer.

There were some days when he himself closely identified with and felt the bitter sorrow in a terrorist's heart. Along with many Japanese, Takuboku was more of a theoretical sympathizer than an active one, while the true terrorist, as given in the poem, has a "heart in which/words and deeds are inseparable", "speaks with deeds/instead of stolen words" and "will sacrifice itself and its body." A taste of faintly bitter cold cocoa is at once the terrorist's and Takuboku's sadness of heart.

These two poems merit special attention because Japan was having her eyes opened for the first time to socialism there at the end of the Meiji Era.

SATŌ HARUO

The Death of a Fool
(from *The Early Poems of Satō Haruo*)

On January 23rd 1911
Ōishi Seinosuke was killed.

Whoever betrays the common law
ought to be killed.

A man who playfully gambled with death;
who, a non-Japanese,
knew nothing of their tribe—
this fool was killed.

On the gallows his last words were the height of folly:
'The truth emerges from a lie.'

My hometown is in the Kishū Shingū district.
So was his.

I hear the towns in the district
were in an uproar.
The wise merchants deplored......

Townsmen, get hold of yourselves!
Teachers, knock some historic sense into the children's heads again!

In 1908 Haruo was called a "delinquent boy" in his hometown (he was sixteen). He wrote some tanka for *Myōjō* (Morning Star) and it was Takuboku who had selected those tanka. That was the only contact they ever had. In 1910-11, however, when anarchists Kōtoku Shūsui and others were being tried for treason in a kangaroo court and suppressed by the government, Haruo and Takuboku were, though at a distance, of one mind.

Ōishi, one member of the coterie who was executed in 1910 (he was a Christian physician) had established a reading room where townsmen could gather to read papers and magazines. He had had the support of his nephew Nishimura Isaku and his minister Takano Iwasaburō with a view to enlightening the townsmen. In his junior high days, Haruo always dropped in coming and going, and read regularly the columns of the *Heimin Shinbun* (The Common Man's Newspaper) or the *Chuō Kōron* magazine.

His young blood boiled. The fact that Kōtoku Shūsui enjoyed boating with Ōishi in Shingū in August 1908 was elicited by the authorities as "proof" that the two of them had conspired to assassinate the Emperor Meiji. The townsmen boggled to observe that Ōishi and four accomplices had grown up among them in such a small town. Haruo, having been introduced to the newspaper through Ōishi's reading room, deeply felt the effect of the entire scandal (even though he was generally said by the townsmen to be a mere delinquent).

In the poem Haruo voices his protest against the authorities by tongue-in-cheek irony concerning Ōishi's "foolishness" and the true foolishness of Shingū's merchant class. He despised his hometown, as young people often do. "The truth emerges from a lie" is found in his written reflections on the Bible which he had read in jail. "Looked at from any point of view, this world is crazy," he wrote. "As Christ says in the seventh verse, "The truth emerges from a lie," and these words truly point to what life is all about." Ōishi's essay went missing for forty years and came to light a few years after the end of World War II.

Serenade on the Road
(from *The Early Poems of Satō Haruo*)

The Emergency Bell rang furiously.
Two guys in their student capes beneath the street lamps
were talking excitedly and one said, 'At least a dozen were killed.'
'Where'll we go—Fukagawa or Asakusa?' the other asked.
An Asakusa-bound train came, sporting a red 'Filled to Capacity'sign.
A woman ran across the tracks!

This poem, too, refers to the 1910 High Treason Incident. It was written a day after the 23rd January execution date. On 18th January they decided on the death sentence for twenty-four of the twenty-six detainees, but on the 19th the Emperor reduced the sentence to life imprisonment for twelve of the condemned. "The Emergency Bell" was rung by way of announcing the execution.

The "two guys" referred to may have been promising young artists such as Haruo himself and Horiguchi Daigaku. These two of course excitedly pored over and discussed the newspaper extra that had appeared. One contained himself well enough to note that as many as a dozen had been executed; the other, his mind racing unconcernedly ahead, was wondering which direction to head in search of a prostitute. The streetcar filled to overflowing and a woman rushing across the tracks suggest nothing unusual and indeed the street scene is typically unremarkable. Ever since the sentence had been passed, six days earlier, one young man had waited and watched breathlessly; the announcement now relieves the tension as though a taut thread had snapped. His hopes that the sentence would be rescinded were exploded for it now became clear that the government was utterly immovable.

TAKAMURA KŌTARŌ

A Bedraggled Ostrich
(from *Beast Poems*)

What's so strange about keeping an ostrich
in a very small room in a muddy zoo?
Ain't its stride too long,
its neck too long?

In this snowy area its feathers will go ragged.
It might get hungry and eat some hard bread
yet its eyes ain't a long, long way away.
Its burning eyes seem to long for water.
It thirsts madly for the onset of an azure wind.
Dreams swirl around in its small, simple brain.
Ain't just an ostrich anymore!

For God's sake,
put an end to this.

This was one of the best of the *Beast Poems*. He knew that an uncontrollable beast dwelled inside of him—something violently wild yet without which people would lose their humanity. Imprisoned in "a very small room in a muddy zoo," the ostrich is a metaphor for the element of mankind's suppressed wildness.

Vast dreams swirl inside the ostrich's "small, simple brain." For an ostrich to be what it is, it must yearn to return to the distant desert where it can be what it is. Kōtarō actually hates the men who have thus denaturized the ostrich. The inelegance of Kōtarō language ("ain't') is an appropriate way to emphasize his indignation.

MIYAZAWA KENJI

3rd November
(from his date book)

I wouldn't want to give in
to wind and rain;
to snow or the heat of summer.
I wish to have a strong body,
no greed,
never to express my indignation,
and always smile quietly.
Every day I'd eat a lot of brown rice,
a little miso and some vegetables.
I'd devote myself
to others.

I want to see more of the world,
understand, and not forget.
I'd live in a thatch-roofed shack
in a pine grove on the field
and when a child on the east got sick
I'd go and take care of him;
when a mother on the west side got tired
I'd take her some sheaves of rice on my back.
In the south when a man was dying
I'd talk him out of his fear,
and when the north neighbors argued and went to court
I'd tell them to stop their nonsense.
I'd shed tears in a spell of dry weather;
I'd fret and idle the time away in a cold summer.
People would call me a bump on a log;
a man
no one would praise or condemn
is the kind of man
I'd like to be.

During Kenji's final and fatal illness he jotted down this sort of poem and other poetic fragments and notes in his notebook. This poem in particular, published posthumously, became quite popular on account of its undeniable passion. We wonder, however, if Kenji intended its publication as a poem. It seems clear that it needed further refinement.

Some people find it a typical Miyazawa poem, though, and its fame was assured by its being used in lower school texts. It is taken for granted that Kenji's ideal man is truly depicted therein; moreover, the poem supposes that Kenji indeed wished to identify with peasants. We should not leap so simply to such conclusions, however. Mr. Nakamura Minoru offers the following detailed comment:

He [Miyazawa] was an agricultural scientist as well as a poet and found great life satisfaction in the former role. In 1926 he established an agricultural society called Rasu Chijin Kyōkai in the suburbs of Hanamaki in Iwate, intending to lecture the young on effective rice production, soil and its improvement, the use of fertilizers and the art of agriculture. He also set up several free clinics to teach the effective use of fertilizers around the various villages. Whenever a cold summer or another disaster was forecast, he went from village to village to organize a counter plan. In August 1928 he exposed himself so recklessly to foul weather, on behalf of others, that he fell ill with a fever... he was forced to stop his work. Although he carried   the program on faithfully for three years, ultimately the project failed. We should read this poem in the context of this major setback. His heartfelt anguish and remorse underlie the lines:

> I'd shed tears in a spell of dry weather;
> I'd fret and idle the time away in a cold summer.
> People would call me a bump on a log.

In consequence his lines are remarkably redolent of the "real."

The opinion given here—Mr. Nakamura's—strikes with pinpoint accuracy, in my view. We should bear in mind of course that this poem was written by an incurable invalid towards the end of his days.

KIYAMA SHŌHEI

Darkness Falls As We Level the Ground
(from *The Poems of Kiyama Shōhei*)

Shimpei got a knockout for a bride.
He said
he'd build a new house,
so we went out and leveled the ground.

Takichi
Rinzō
Yonesaku
Okoyo
......
......
We villagers got together and sang songs
keeping the beat with clapping.
Stomping

stomping
to a *Yo-ho* !
Ropes in hand
we tugged and pulled
one for all, all as one.
Stomping
stomping
to a *Yo-ho* !
One long day in spring
we stomped and leveled, and darkness fell.

This poem, obviously, deals with the villagers' collaboration in building a new home for a newly-married couple. The original's verb "*shintaku suru*" (lit. "new-made build") may well be from a local dialect. The feeling is carefree as they pound and level the ground. The original title literally means "pounding the earth"—a phrase that makes us chuckle.

NAKAHARA CHŪYA

At Noon
—A View of the Marunouchi Building—
(from *Songs of Bygone Days*)

Ah! There goes the noon bell! The bell!
The people spill and stumble out.
Salaried folks hurry out;
They keep on filing out en masse from
a tiny black hole in that huge building.
The broad sky is a bit cloudy and dust is swirling everywhere.
Looking on with disbelieving eyes
I feel like a misplaced cherry blossom.
Ah! There goes the noon bell! The bell!
The people spill and stumble out.
Tiny black holes in great buildings.
The bell echoes, reverberates, vanishes in the wind.

This was to be Chūya's last poem published in his lifetime. A typical lunch-time scene, people pour out like long lines of black ants. The original brings a light touch to the traditional syllabic rhythm, which therefore creates an ironic tone that subtly makes fun of the white collar workers. They come off as aimless and insipid. Of all Chūya's poems this is the most understandable and comical; the one that city dwellers understand all too well about a situation in which they are helpless. At the same time it is a highly rhythmical poem. For these very reasons the poem is much appreciated by everyone.

NAKANO SHIGEHARU (1886-1943)

Farewell before Daybreak
(from *The Poems of Nakano Shigeharu*)

We've got to begin.
We've got to talk it through.
Of course the cops will come
and smash our eyes and noses.
That's why we have to keep switching rooms,
rooms with access to back doors and alleys.

Six of us young guys sleep in this room;
a couple and their baby are downstairs.
I know nothing about the lives of these six;
it's just that we're comrades.
I don't know the downstairs couple's name.
I only know they cheerfully let us use this room.

It's near dawn.
We'll probably switch rooms again,
carrying our satchels,
talking things over,
and carrying on the job.
We'll sleep on another rental futon tomorrow night.

It's near dawn.
This tiny room,
diapers strung on a cord,
a sooty naked bulb,
a celluloid toy,
rented futon,
fleas—

I say goodbye to all of you.
That flowers should bloom!
Our flowers.
One for the couple downstairs
and their baby.
Let them all together burst into bloom.

In former times when the leftist movement was outlawed followers had to seek out obscure or hidden quarters for their consultations. The term was coined, "kaigō o motsu," which smacks of translation from a foreign language. When the owner of a house used by the leftists fell under suspicion the police, always on the lookout, called upon him. Since the risk was so great, activists were always on the move.

The poem's "couple" were indeed kind people; even the activists knew absolutely nothing about them. They knew only that they were recipients of a great kindness ("We should be mutually supportive," etc.). The activists were always on the move. Out of this encounter—once and once only—a heartrending affection was born.

OGUMA HIDEO (1901-1940)

I Wish I Were Thinking in the Body of a Horse
(from *The Poems of a Wanderer*)

Ah, my hometown horse,
in the cradle next to you
I learned my first words,
as many words as there were villagers.
I left the village and became a poet
so I needed a lot of words
and got to know very many
that ordinary people didn't.
I tried to speak for the people.
From sluggish words like 'monster tank'
to swift words like 'lightning,'
freedom of speech was mine—
not anyone else's.
But suddenly a great thief said,
'Shut up!

Pipe down!'
drawing a knife under my nose.
I who had once been so outspoken
lost courage and strength.
Gradually I became a shell of a man.
I cursed my unlucky star
for not having been born dumb.
I no longer wanted to have this human shape.
Oh, hometown horse,
I wish I were thinking all the time
in your body.
If I couldn't speak naturally
even just the word 'freedom'
then on some icy-cold night,
my horse, breathing, like you,
white steam from my nostrils,
I'd like to return to my cold town.

Hideo died in poverty at thirty-nine. Around 1937 as the situation deteriorated leftist men of letters gradually had their publishing rights undercut, suffered from dire poverty and began to find blood in their phlegm (tuberculosis was rife).

As a rule Hideo's poetic lines are fluid but garrulous and over-composed. His "Keep on Talking" in its very title represents that trend. Suddenly, however, his poems were adjudged anathema. For a poet who had enjoyed freedom of speech silence was an intolerable insult. "I no longer wanted to have this human shape." brings a lump to the throat.

KANEKO MITSUHARU

On the Day of My Son's Conscription Examination
(from *The Moth*)

It causes more desperation
than leprosy would.
Taken away by force,
threatened,
sworn in,

the young men are lined up and certified
(my son among them).

How is it, Ken-chan?
You used to be a little gentleman.
You, you Hellenist,
have to give yourself up for lost.
There's no way around
this long wall,
no way to preserve your pinch of freedom
in a cookie jar.
Yet, my shy, weak son,
lined up like the others,
don't give in!
Like a clean-planed, thin board
you stand newly naked.
Your distant father, so far away,
is watching fearfully,
nodding,
smiling.
You're like a frail, thin reed
standing in the dark waters of Japan;
everything around you has been swept away,
and you find yourself in an unthinkable place.
Even in such a swift torrent
you who tremble in resistance,
you who, taken away, will never return,
you my only son,
you without whom my life is bereft,
this foolish father stares at you,
longs not to lose you,
longs to take you back.
And silently you say words you said before:
—Impossible! We're lost!
Those guys are out-Heroding Herod
to a man—infanticide—
their actions as capricious
as the decisions of the Convention.

Mitsuharu's poem "Mt. Fuji" (cf. the next section, "Nature") concerns the military call-up of his oldest son Ken. The above poem concerns the physical exam proper. Today's young people are unfamiliar with this practice. In the last stages of the war, conscription call-ups greatly multiplied, but just before that time all young men of twenty had to take the exam. Evasion was a serious crime.

The poem "Mt. Fuji" is filled with the deep sorrow Mitsuharu felt when his son, called up, was essentially bound to die. The above poem is also, to be sure, filled with the same sorrow and yet he maintains objectivity enough to ask ironically, "How is it, Ken-chan?" This line introduces at least a light touch; however, at that time the physical exam filled people with despair, because conscription meant being drafted or sent to the front. Comparing his son to a reed in dark waters, the poet gazes despondently at his son's back as he walks away. We hear voices complaining indignantly at such jingoism as "to a man" and complaining over the capriciousness of the state's power, along with a voice that cries out in sorrow for "the apple of his eye."

HARA TAMIKI (1905-1951)

these are human beings
(from *The Poems of Hara Tamiki*)

these are human beings.
look at how the atomic bomb has altered them.
their bodies are horribly bloated.
both men and women are reduced to one shape,
oh, burned black, wrecked,
charred faces; and from their swollen lips
fall faint, feeble voices:
help me, please!
these are human beings,
human faces.

Tamiki's short story collection *Summer Flowers* brought to light for the first time his direct experience of the katakana syllabary [a syllabary normally reserved for the transcribing of non-Japanese words]. He claimed that the only way in which he could mollify the pain he felt over the atrocious bombing was to write it in katakana. Even his own poems incorporated in the story are in katakana.

The horror of the bombing made him determined to present purely documentary poems, free of personal bias. Katakana somehow enabled him to hit upon apt phrases. The poem above is one of those. It gives concise expression to the atrocity he could not otherwise give voice to; the choice of words is deliberate; they have a natural authority about them. Other poets might have spoken in greater realistic detail—Tamiki could not.

KINOSHITA YŪJI (1914-1965)

The Memory of Fire
—on the anniversary of the atomic bombing of Hiroshima—
(from *The Poems of Kinoshita Yūji*)

However tenderly vines extend their hands
from under the hedgerow by the house,
they cannot catch that cloud.
Though it seems to be floating close by
it is far, too far away.

One dying cicada chirring feebly
in a treetop suddenly dies
and a surrounding host of them
just as suddenly sing out in concert.

On a street corner
or at a grade crossing on a country road
I stop and step on my shadow.

However far away the sun may travel
and even though the shadows engraved
on stone pavements on that day may disappear,
still more strongly, heavily, madly I step on my own shadow.

Since Yūji was born and was living in Fukuyama (in the eastern part of Hiroshima Prefecture), he did not directly experience the atomic bomb. His information came from witnesses and victims, the disaster- stricken city being not too distant.

On every 8th August following the bombing, a ceremony called "Prayer for World Peace," has been carried out in a not wholly sincere manner. The ceremony is irrelevant to the atomic bomb disaster. Needless to say, "that cloud" refers to the huge, familiar mushroom.

When he stops and steps on his own shadow, some memories are revived: shadows imprinted on the concrete around the city. Recalling those shadows in fear and trembling, he tries all the more strongly to trample on his own shadow.

MIYOSHI TATSUJI

A Tiny, Tiny Elephant is Here
(from *Astride a Camel's Humps*)

Typhoon and flood have come;
to Tokyo, Japan, autumn.
A tiny, tiny elephant is here,
two and a-half years old,
a big fat baby.

The elephant is a lovable creature,
even more lovable for being a baby.
It arrived on a straw bed
in a freight car munching bananas
and sweet potatoes, and napping.

A tiny, tiny elephant is here.
Since a cow has no tusks,
this one's an *elephas maximus.**
Of course it'll offer its trunk
and shake hands with us.

Crossing the boundless ocean
from Bangkok to Tokyo,
what did it dream,
waving its innocent trunk?
A tiny, tiny elephant is here.

A tiny, tiny elephant is here.
When it comes to presents,
a light trunk is also perfectly fitting.
Is it because it's fall here in Tokyo

that the wind is bone-chilling?
A tiny, tiny elephant is here.

*The Asian cow elephant has no tusks. This elephant was the gift of a Thai merchant.
The *Nichi Nichi* newspaper (*Day-to-Day*) stated that the baby as it marched down the
Ginza was roundly applauded. It was named Hanako.

In 1949, on 1st September, a female Thai elephant was landed in Kōbe. A
freight car transported it to Shimbashi Station and from there it marched down
Shōwa Street to Ueno Zoo to a tumultuous reception. During the war all the
large or dangerous animals had been disposed of and so the country was
completely without elephants. Tatsuji was outraged by the loud welcome given
the elephant; he thought that in this manner the people revealed their
dispiritedness following defeat in the war. The devastated Japanese military
was, he thought, a deplorable development.

Tatsuji's indignant lamentation in its own satirical way depicts the atmosphere
of post-war days. The 5- 7 syllabic line combination is a fixed form that seems
right for the elephant as object and for Tatsuji's satirical purpose. It would be
appropriate to read "Nippon, Tokyo" (Japan, Tokyo) with a foreigner's accent.

AMANO TADASHI (1909-1993)

Rice
(from *A Simple Lifetime*)

Pick up these grains of rice
scattered about the wet railroad tracks,
will you?
It's a sort of rice-bomb sack
thrown out of the train window near the station.

Rice grains spilled from the sack.
Pick up these rain soaked grains
scattered around the tracks, will you?
Bring me the woman bearer
who was manhandled and hauled away a little while ago,
and please ask her, her husband forced into the front lines
and killed, how she managed
to raise her children, no money or anything else.
And ask her if her children

had ever had enough rice to eat.
Ask her gently, before God and man.
These rice grains shining in the rain and mud
were raised up by some
stupidly honest, poor Japanese peasant.
Pick up those grains of rice, will you?

Pick them up one by one,
silently.

Soon after the war ended some people were "self-employed" in the black market rice industry. If caught with such rice, dealers were of course immediately arrested by the police; if they knew they were under surveillance they could do nothing but throw the rice sack out of the train window and try to escape. A rice sack would break open and grains would be broadcast all around.

Such scenes were repeated daily. It was all but impossible to eliminate the black market and police raids occurred constantly. This poet expresses his indignation over the situation in which Japanese found themselves.

IBARAGI NORIKO (1926-)

When I was at My Most Beautiful
(from *Dialogue*)

When I was at my most beautiful
the cities were all bombed and burned out
but I could see the blue sky
in quite unexpected places.

When I was at my most beautiful
many people died
in factories, on the seas and nameless islands.
I lost my incentive to be fashionable.

When I was at my most beautiful
no one gave me presents at all.
Men knew nothing but the military salute.
They were gone, leaving only their admiring glances.

When I was at my most beautiful
I stopped thinking.
My heart turned hard,
my arms and legs shone like chestnuts.

When I was at my most beautiful
my country lost the war.
I couldn't believe it. Instead I
rolled up my sleeves and strutted down the defeated streets.

When I was at my most beautiful
and jazz poured from the radio,
I relished the sweet, exotic music
and felt giddy as when, forbidden, I first began to smoke.

When I was at my most beautiful
I felt utterly unhappy.
There was never a meeting of minds
and that left me terribly lonely.

So I decided to live as long as possible,
like an old Rouault
who in his old age painted most gloriously.
You know?

Noriko spent her adolescence in the confused war and post-war years. Her beauty in those years shone in vain.

She writes as follows about civilian labor conscription during the war:

The Sea of Nebukawa

Slim and pale though I was
I embraced this country,
bearing up......
A small girl in overalls
in my salad days—
Ah, Sea of Nebukawa,
you won't forget?

The tone of these lines quite differs from that of "When I was at My Most Beautiful." If these lines are melancholic, "When I was at My Most Beautiful" is somewhat cheerful and is gay enough to dispel melancholy. The war years were truly miserable for women to live through, yet strangely the tone behind "I felt utterly unhappy" is a light-hearted one, as when one hums a tune. It probably reveals her deep intention to let bygones be bygones and to live a long time.

ANZAI HITOSHI (1919-1994)

A Lonely Village
(from *A Cherry Tree in Blossom*)

It's so comforting to see
that young man
walking around the house
fixing the snow-sodden roof
and the radio antenna, chopping firewood,
polishing the stove and storing it in the barn,
filling the environs
with the air of youth,
the sweat on his chest glittering in the sun.

Some ne'er-do-well husband died an alcoholic.
His hard-working son was killed in the war.
The men had all gone off to die.
For no good reason
they all disappeared in a hurry.
Only the women endlessly endure.
The village is crowded with widows and crows.
Hey, let's go, you young stud.
You're the only hold-out.
You hot young stud,
you lonely left-over tough guy.

How lonely I feel
watching this young guy
working around the house.
Humming, thumping the slushy ground,
he goes after a drink of water.

In the shade of the barn or even by the well
he'll finish his work and rape you.
But in this village of widows and crows,
there's nothing left but a bunch of barren women.

A desolate village is pictured when in the post-war years the young men are either all dead or have migrated to the city. A widow-narrator opens the poem with a monologue as in a reverie.

Since the surviving men could not make a living in the village they went to live in temporary shacks in the city as day laborers. Yet once in the city they disappeared without a trace. Widows and crows alone remain in the village. Farming was dependent solely on grandfather, grandmother, and mother (this was called "3-chan farming" in the press, the three names all followed by the affectionate term "chan"—for "san"; that is to say, Grandpa, Grandma and Mom). Scholars also regularly discussed the depopulation of farm villages.

Towards the poem's end the widow's reverie still continues ("In the shade of the barn...."). She imagines that women are easily seduced and yet she feels how dreary and empty the world is where the wild males are gone and nothing remains "but a bunch of barren women." What the widow has imagined resembles a picture-scroll of hell.

VI

Nature

KUNIKIDA DOPPO (1871-1908)

Freedom Dwells in Mountains and Forests
(from *Recitations by Doppo*)

My blood is deeply stirred when I say,
'Freedom dwells in mountains and forests.'
Ah, freedom dwells in mountains and forests.
Why have I forsaken them?

Ten years have passed since, longing for the city,
I came and wandered its vain roads.
Looking back at the freedom of my early days
I feel as if I have come to the opposite end of the road.

While looking reverently at the distant heavens
I behold the morning sun cast its partial shadow
on the lofty, snowy peaks. My blood is stirred when I say,
'Freedom dwells in mountains and forests.'

Where now is my beloved hometown?
There I could be the son of mountains and forests.
Mountains and rivers now seem a thousand miles away.
My hometown freedom vanishes into the clouds.

In fact Doppo is really at his best in the short story where his poetic sensibility is brought to richer fruition. Strongly influenced by the English Lake poet Wordsworth, he sang paeans to nature in which he found true freedom. Mountains and forests are the antithesis of "vain roads," which is to say "life in the city." Having given up the mountains and forests of his hometown, he deeply regrets his immersion in the hustle and bustle of the city. He is obsessed with the fear that his hometown freedom has vanished from the earth.

This, of his very few poems, is considered representative. Because he makes a special use of Japanese words of Chinese origin ("kango"), the poem is rhythmically strong and expresses his romantic sentiment *viva voce*.

TAKAMURA KŌTARŌ

Deep Snow Banks
(from *Paragons*)

Deep snow banks defined level lanes through the pine grove.
I sank knee-deep.
The snow emitted a phosphorescence
in the faint sunlight,
a pale blue hue, like sea-fire.
Across the lane I spotted sporadic rabbit tracks
that disappeared into the darkening grove.
Just ten steps and I had to recover my breath;
twenty steps and I fell to my knees.
Snow alighted pathetically on still treetops
and made me want to write a poem.
The clouds had already crystallized into mountain peaks.
But what of my unformed poem?
I lighted some dry cedar boughs,
meaning to heat up my rice porridge.
For a man like me staring defeat in the face,
something glistened in my soul, easing my anxiety.
The beauty of it I could not quite take hold of.

In October 1945 Kōtarō moved to a shabby cabin in Ōta Village in the Hienuki District of Iwate Prefecture. Out of a sense of self-loathing for his speech and behavior during the war he tried to banish himself, into the mountains. In that snow country, autumn was over in a flash and the heavy snows fell and fell.

Where was he going, we wonder, knee-deep in the snow? "...ten steps and I had to recover my breath" and "twenty steps and I fell to my knees"—here, an aging poet of sixty-three, short-winded, had to keep walking as long as he lived. "Across the lane I spotted rabbit tracks/that disappeared into the darkening grove." struck him as a scene of frozen other-worldly beauty. Snow reflected phosphorescence and his serene soul was surrounded by a similar—and untouchable—sparkle and glitter. This, after the end of great sorrow, was peace of mind. We can imagine his sorrow fading off into an unknown, hazy darkness.

MURŌ SAISEI

I Understand Suppressed Feelings
(from *Cranes*)

I love an endless expanse of ice,
the suppressed feelings it imposes.
I've seen its rainbow-shining.
I love flowers (except flowery flowers).
Something deep down in ice attracts me.
I am drawn by things deep down, blade-sharp.
My life is peculiarly narrow.
I groan under the onus of it.
That's why I love an endless expanse of ice,
the suppressed feelings it imposes.

This poem Saisei selected for inscribing on a stele in Karuizawa erected while he still lived. All the more because he felt he lived a desolate life he claimed to love an "endless expanse of ice." The world as lukewarm or bland is a notion utterly at odds with the constructive, compressed, hardened feelings suggested by something "blade-sharp" and "deep down." Here we can perceive the sharp edge of Saisei's sensitivity as he finds something compatible in "an endless expanse of ice."

MUSHANOKŌJI SANEATSU

Ode to a Persimmon
(from *The Poems of Mushanokōji Saneatsu*)

No one notices persimmon flowers,
they're so inconspicuous;
yet the fruits are conspicuous
and are celebrated.

They are so sweet
we can't help saying so;
but stopping to think about it,
I myself don't think they're so sweet.

'I, like everyone else,
have been pummeled by wind and rain
and been frozen, like everyone else,
by frost and snow.
But I've eaten manna
and gathered the dewdrops of heaven,
and produced my fruit.'

'I've never been pummeled by dewdrops of manna
nor taken root in the fount of manna dew,   ·
yet I have secreted dewdrops from my very center.'

And I—am I the same?

Saneatsu writes in praise of the source of life. "I"—the persimmon tree (in
stanzas 3-4)—"have been pummeled by wind and rain". "I" has been "frozen"
but has never needed outside sustenance because that has come from within.
The overflowing inner source of life has enabled him to produce admirable
fruit. Nature's will is powerful and wonderful beyond human imagining.

The "I" (of stanzas 4-5)—the poet—asks whether he is like the persimmon
tree.

NAKA KANSUKE (1885-1965)

The Siberian Meadow-Bunting
(from *Crystalline Pebbles*)

Chi-chin Chi-chin Chi-ri-ko-ro-ro
In the grove
among innumerable pines,
the white-cheeked bunting sings, his voice
ringing out like a small bell.
Patches of snow
still remain on the mountain,
but beyond—ah!—spring has come.

Chi-chin Chi-chin Chi-ri-ko-ro-ro

I used to make a pilgrimage to Shinano
to forget a maiden I could not forget.
In my loneliness I strolled around the foxtail millet fields
by the lake in a mountain village.
The birdsong from millet-ears—
chi-chin-ko-ro-ri-ya—
reminded me of my vanished youth.
The song was as beautiful as dreaming.

This affectionate little piece of poetry in homage to the bunting is rhythmically reminiscent of a nursery rhyme. In the bunting's song Kansuke hears a foretelling of the summer that is approaching across the mountains. The birdsong tempted him to indulge in his own precious retrospection. The trip to Shinano was by way of forgetting a girl; however, spotting the bunting in the field, he at once recalled the girl's white countenance. Its plaintive song put him in mind of his long-vanished and irreplaceable love.

This is one of two poems he wrote on the same subject (the other one, "The Voices of the Siberian Meadow Bunting", reads, in part, "Ah, I am alone,/all alone./It feels good, alone like this./Good, being alone for good."). He had lived long as a bachelor—indeed he did not marry until 1942, at fifty-seven.

YAMAMURA BOCHŌ (1884-1924)

River in Spring
(from *Clouds*)

I wonder whether
the river sweeps along
continuously
or not.
The morning clouds,
afloat,
speak for themselves.

Clouds

Hey, clouds,
you look free
and easy-going.

where are you headed?
As far as Iwakidaira?

In the collection *Clouds* can be seen Bochō's final poetic phase. That is why I chose these two little poems. He writes "The poorer I become at writing poems, the more delighted I really am." He sought to listen to what he called "the deep-down voice of nature." Every *Clouds* poem, though he was a minister, seems to indicate that, withal, he had become a pantheist. In fact, in order to make a living, at that time he had to write fairy tales and children's songs and thus by extension his poems resemble children's songs that are filled with human wonder at nature. Although he appears to aim at a calculated effect, in these poems there is decidedly evident a preference for the Japanese beauty of brevity.

OZAKI KIHACHI (1892-1974)

A Song from Kiso
–The Torii Pass–
(from *Songs of Time and Tide*)

Grabbing roots and rocks to help us, panting and sweating,
we climb up the overgrown, unused Nakasendō Trail.
The songs of the Siberian Blue Robin above the trail
and the Arctic Warbler below
penetrate the deep mountain's noon silence.

For hundreds of years a virgin forest of horse chestnuts
stood near the Pass. Their top white blossoms ascended skyward.
Moss and decayed trees scented the downward slope.
The Nutcracker sang softly, huskily;
a Green Woodpecker flew off with a shrill cry.

The view expanded
as we reached the top of the old Pass.
Glittering hot air wavered in the dale.
Above the dream-like, vast Mt. Kiso-Ontake,
a dozen miles distant, a summer mist spread over the valley.

Cicada song deafened us.
With eyes and ears we observed the recital
of one cicada perched on a stone monument.
In focus, the insect sang and inched forward; out of focus,
beyond the monument, the river flowed silvery by old Yabuhara Station.

The love relation between Kihachi and mountains began in 1928 when at thirty-six he met and climbed with a mountaineer named Kawada Miki. He was won over by their beauty.

As a boy he had been uncommonly interested in flora and fauna; the attraction to mountains thus came only later. His innate interest in nature or the interest he acquired as a young boy was awakened under the influence of the White Birch writers and other men of letters, and by poets such as Takamura Kōtarō.

This poem, written in Kiso, is almost from beginning to end a psalm in praise of the natural world along the Kiso Road. We can almost hear Kihachi gasping for breath as he climbs the deserted narrow path of Nakasendō (this path fed into Nakasendō as one leg of the Kiso Road, one of the five major roads of Japan). The pleasures found as he strolls through this magnificent natural setting we, too, keenly feel.

The Torii Pass is the only spot along the Kiso road which commands a view of Mt. Kiso-Ontake. Kihachi states that "to think about Kiso is to think about the beauty of simplicity in the human heart." The poem leads us along an untrodden path; only a few kinds of birds appear. Immersing himself in these mountains cut through by the Kiso River, he grows increasingly awed. As he spiritually descends into the depths of nature in these breath-taking moments, we find him profoundly grateful for the days of his life.

NAKANO SHIGEHARU

A Song
(from *The Poems of Nakano Shigeharu*)

Don't sing!
Don't sing about little red flowers or dragonflies' wings
or wind whispering or the scent of women's hair.
Get rid of everything unreal,
all glaring lies

and all things tedious.
Get rid of all mere appearances.
Sing songs of simple honesty,
something edible,
something that pulses in your heart.
Songs whose beat beats on and on,
songs that draw courage from a well of shame.
Sing these songs to an austere melody,
full-throated.
Press these songs upon
everybody's heart.

This poem was interpreted to mean that Shigeharu rejected simple "nature" poems. Behind ll.2-3 lies the fact that the poet is keenly attracted to natural things, so we believe that he had long held "nature" in high esteem.

There is after all a pathetic way of writing about red flowers, dragonflies' wings and the like that produces fake feelings. Fixed patterns of melodies abounded in haiku, tanka and popular songs—almost clichés. In this poem he expressed the judgement that he himself has never tried to write in such a false way.

He insists on singing "songs of simple honesty,/something edible". Takuboku's *Poems to Eat* at once comes to mind. In spite of his intention—no, all the more for that—Takuboku tried in his tanka, arranged in three-line segments, to capture the fleeting emotions of the moment. And no one will say that they are "unreal" or "glaring lies."

To rise to a superficial fever pitch about red flowers and dragonflies' wings was something Shigeharu found abominable. Possessed of this disposition, he writes in negative imperatives: "Don't.... Don't...." He knows, however, that in the onrush of daily life one can in the process of neglecting nature grow corrupt.

MIYOSHI TATSUJI

Great Mt. Aso
(from *The Cape in Spring*)

Horses are standing in the rain.
In the rain, horses and a few foals.

Silently, silently, the rain.
The horses are grazing.
Their tails, backs and manes soaked through,
they're grazing.
Some merely stand, heads lowered.
The rain is falling, silently, silently.
Smoke is rising from the mountain,
thin yellow billows rising heavy-hearted
from the peak of Nakadake.
Clouds spread across the sky,
the rain unsure whether to work or play.
Horses grazing on a rain-washed hill
of a pasture in Kusasenri-hama,
grazing intently.
There they stand grazing.
Soaking wet, they graze silently forever.
This moment could be
a hundred years.
Rain, falling, rain,
silent, silent rain....

Tatsuji had climbed Mt. Aso in the rain one day in 1937. What he saw was a gloriously, somehow eerily timeless sight, those horses grazing on the hillside with Mt. Nakadake exhaling smoke in the background. The atmosphere enfolds us; we feel wrapped in a moment of eternity. "This moment could be/a hundred years." refers to the eternality of nature and are the only lines in the poem not written in the present active tense.

The "standing, grazing, rising, falling" verbals are quite effective here, such that the one deviant tense stands out all the more. The scenery is frozen in a moment of time so that now or a hundred years later the scenery is as ever. Turning plain-spoken words to advantage, the poem condenses a century into one moment—one moment in which, body and soul, we can be immersed in the vastness of the natural world.

KUSANO SHIMPEI

Mt. Fuji
(from *Mt. Fuji*)

The river is dazzled by spring light...the breeze blows light
...reeds whisper...
a Great Reed Warbler chirps, its tongue a-light with spring.

White clover grows to the bank.
I cup my chin in my hands,
looking about languidly
in a shower of spring light.

Girls fashion white clover into garlands and ropes, and jump,
Fuji-san framed in the arc of the rope
over and over, near, framed, unframed....

The Warbler's song in my ear,
the light of spring on my cheeks....

Ever since the 8th century when Yamabe-no-Akahito wrote about Mt. Fuji, Japanese poets and painters have sung, in paint and poetry, its praises. Now in the 1960s, such painters as Yokoyama Taikan, Umehara Ryūzaburō and Hayashi Takeshi are famous for their paintings of this mountain; among poets, Shimpei's work is particularly known. The poem above is one of an entire collection on Mt. Fuji. It is a poetic prologue to the book.

The setting is a river bank brilliantly illuminated by the light of spring; a reed warbler is chirping and children are innocently romping. Sitting on a bed of white clover by the bank, the poet, who has been somewhat melancholy, relaxes and watches the scene. Girls are weaving garlands and making a jump rope. The swung rope at its apogee is filled with a Mt. Fuji that draws near; at its nadir, the mountain recedes.

Katsushika Hokusai once made a print of Mt. Fuji as framed in and seen through a huge barrel of sorts [that was used for other purposes]. Another of his prints shows a giant wave breaking and, framed under the arch of it, Fuji-san in the distance. In this poem Shimpei encircles distant Fuji-san in a rope of white clover. The mountain is drawn in bright spring sunlight with children vibrantly alive.

KANEKO MITSUHARU

Mt. Fuji
(from *The Moth*)

In this sardine can called Japan
there isn't room enough to swing a cat.

The nation is oppressive everywhere.
We're always watched.

And they have the gall to call us up
for military duty.

The official family registry be damned!
Forget I have a son!

Hey, son,
Let me hide you in my hand
or hide you in the depths of my hat.

Your mother and I were talking things over
all night in an inn at the foot of a mountain.

Rain soaked the dead trees,
cracking against limbs and trunks.
It fell all night long.

Son, you're sopping wet,
walking, panting, dragging a heavy rifle,
almost unconscious—where are you?

But your Dad and Mom will go looking for you
wherever we have to go.
A horrible, long and restless night of dreams
has finally ended.

The rain has stopped at last.
The blank sky.....
and my son will go away.

What crap, Mt. Fuji standing there
like a shabby gown.

Mt. Fuji sometimes does not come in for praise. It is disgust rather than admiration that comes through in the image of the "shabby gown." The soaring mountain, a national symbol, is held in contempt.

The red-paper summons arrives for the son, who is then seen off by his parents who at this time feel unspeakable animosity toward the State and are filled with prayers for his safety. They are overpowered by dreadful dreams; they are sleepless. When they awake to find the incessant rain at last stopped, they behold Mt. Fuji in the "blank sky" posing in tremendous self-importance.

KURAHARA SHINJIRŌ (1899-1965)

Yesterday's Image
(from *A Char*)

A praying mantis on the edge of unconsciousness
raises its axes high above the horizon
and, gazing at the swift clouds,
clings to the tip of a stalk
and sways.

As the horizon catches the last light of the sun,
there are reflected in its glassy blue eyes
the specks of a gossamer wing
and thistles swaying in the distance.

Those are yesterday as it was.

A praying mantis is still alive—barely—in the desolate, withered weeds, camouflaged by a dry stalk. The dying eyes show a blue that fades into pale brown in its last moments on the stalk. L.1 is certainly an unusual observation. What it saw in its dimming consciousness was reflected in its "glassy blue eyes". With these images held in its heart, the mantis will die. The figure there on the verge of death is excruciatingly beautiful.

MARUYAMA KAORU

A Fox
(from *The North Country*)

They say a fox never gets his tail wet.
Even fleeing a hunter or a bear,
he crosses a mountain torrent
and never a drop of water touches his tail,
so deftly he wields that heavy bushy tail.

One day somewhere I saw a fox
carefully crossing a rapids
and just before he cleared it—
too bad! Dame Fortune bedeviled him.
His tail brushed the water's surface.

In that very instant he jumped as though attacked,
sped off to hide in the evening mist,
though beyond the mist I could momentarily see
how chagrinned he was,
writhing, running in deep remorse.

Does a fox actually behave in such a way? I don't know and it doesn't matter even if it doesn't, because Mr. Maruyama's description is wonderful.

The archaism "Dame Fortune" creates, to the contrary, a happy effect in this poem. The fox's blunder, though undeniably comical, briefly amuses us but then we stop chuckling and feel a sort of loneliness. The fox's remorse and shame become ours. And I am persuaded, "Well, *C'est la vie.*"

TORIMI HAYAHIKO (1910- 1990)

A Different Night
(from *The Untrodden Path*)

Half-way down a cliff
I hang suspended
with no purchase on these unwieldy rocks.
I secure myself to the rope and hang there.

The sun has set,
today's journey
complete.
A terrible night begins.

So night is lonely?
Bitter?
Scary?
Don't complain. You made your own bed.

Fearful and remorseful....
Between miscalculation and longing
while I sway and sway, I scold and pardon myself.
It's a ghastly night.

I can't even see any village lights.
No light that binds people.
A world unfamiliar, distant from the normal world.
A lonely, cold, cruel night.

Hayahiko was a mountaineer and poet. The poem's situation is almost unimaginably formidable. At mid-point on the cliff he binds himself to a rope and hangs suspended, just as the horribly fearful night sets in. In the midst of his precarious swaying, and quite afraid, he tries to remind himself that it was his choice. He tries to accept the fact and to get some sleep. "A Different Night" indicates a lonely, bitter, frightful night under a strange sky far away from town or village.

TANIKAWA SHUNTARŌ (1931-)

A Lie in the Sky
(from *Poems Concerning Love*)

A bird flies delightedly across the sky.
The sky, as it flies, spreads delightfully.
And a man alone, looking up—
who will help him?

A plane unzips and exposes the sky's back,
as if trying to embarrass her.
A man destroys
whatever he sees in the sky.

A bird with its gentle wings
is salving the wound the plane has inflicted.
The bird knows nothing of the sky's lie,
and so all the more the sky is for the bird.

'The sky is blue. Empty.
Empty. Yet because of the sky, birds fly.'

The light rhythmic wit aptly sets off the colloquial freedom of the language. In another poem ("The Bird") Shuntarō states that "The bird doesn't name the sky./It just flies." The relation is clearly symbiotic. On the other hand, sky and airplane are perhaps antithetical, for the plane will expose, humiliate, wound or kill the sky later, while the bird with "tender wings" will heal the sky.

The bird is ignorant of the sky's lie as revealed by the plane and yet its ignorance does not impair its ability to fly. Though man has knowledge, he cannot know the close relationship enjoyed by bird and sky. Mere knowledge is vain. Human wisdom and judgement mean nothing in the face of Nature's harmony and provisioning.

VII

The Soul of a Traveller

SHIMAZAKI TŌSON

At an Old Castle in Komoro
(from *Young Herbs*)

At an old castle in Komoro
a traveller is saddened by white clouds.
The young chickweed hasn't sprouted yet,
the young grasses aren't ready,
for the melting snow has only begun moving
under the sun along the hill's silvery blanket.

The sun is warming but I cannot yet catch
any field fragrance.
Spring is thinly veiled in mist
out there where the wheat still shows green.
Some travellers, still specks, are hurrying
along the path that cuts through the field.

Mt. Asama disappears in darkness.
Someone in Saku is playing a plaintive grass reed.
I pass along the river, watching the waves,
and climb to the tea house along its banks
where, quite alone, I drink cheap sake.
I soon sprawl on the grass and sleep.

The original title of the poem was "The Heart of a Traveller"; it was published in the first number of *The Morning Star* (April 1900). He had gone to Komoro exactly a year earlier to begin teaching in Komoro Gijuku School. Even at the age of twenty-eight he was still single and a man regarding himself as a wanderer who was incapable of giving up his wanderlust. The poem's underlying motif is that of a melancholy traveller who, no longer immature, chanced to drop by an isolated town where he found an old castle beside the Chikuma River.

In that same year he got married and settled down to his teaching job. In 1900 he began writing such prose works as *Sketches of the Chikuma River* and took his first steps as a novelist. Marriage changed him from a wandering poet into a family-oriented novelist.

The poem above and the poem that follows, written about the same time, are notable as the final fruition of his poetic output.

Lord Komuro in the Juei Era—1182-84—ruled over the castle in a line of the prior Lords Takeda, Sengoku and Makino. Around the bend of the river the three remaining gates clearly suggest the former grandeur of the castle.

When the weather begins to warm up in early spring the hills are still splotched with snow, the chickweed still not visible. Tōson the traveller stands disconsolate in one wing of the ruins, nor have we any need to ask why he feels as he does. As long as a man lives, that special sorrow will visit him and wound his heart.

Out in the field he sees some travellers hurrying along the path through the fields. His wound is compounded by the sight of their backs as they disappear and by the plaintive melody of a distant grass reed. "A grass reed in Saku," he thinks, because he is standing in the Saku Basin in the Saku District. The reed is particularly plaintive because this is a site where for centuries warriors rose and fell.

In a tea house he sips some local sake for comfort. He fancies himself following in the wake of those earlier travellers Saigyō and Bashō. Mr. Yoshida Seiichi tells us that Tōson's poem echoes Bashō's haiku:

> A mound of summer grass,
> heroic deeds—
> are these but passing dreams?

Bashō had looked down upon the great Kitakami River from Takadachi, Yoshitsune's High Fort. And Tōson's also then recalls Tu Fu's famous "Looking at Springtime" which directly influenced Bashō's haiku. Rather than mere travelling, a journey was life itself: a cloud floating from nowhere to nowhere.

Song of a Traveller along the Chikuma River
(from *Fallen Plums*)

> Like yesterday,
> today, too, will pass.
> I ask myself,
> 'Why are you so worried about tomorrow?'

I sometimes go down into a vale
where life's ups and downs stir before me;
I look at the indecisive waves of the river
that bring in the sands and sweep them out again.

Ah, you ruins of the old castle, what will you say?
And you waves washing in, what will you answer?
Seriously ponder the past and you find
a hundred years ago seems only yesterday.

Mist blurs the willows along the shore.
Spring, and the waters are shallow.
Roaming alone among the rocks,
I feel loneliness.

Compared to the former poem, "Song" exudes a more dismal outlook on life. Seized by many emotions, the poet, feeling life's immutable swiftness, feels that "a hundred years ago seems only yesterday." Does Tōson find in the waves' indecision a token of human sorrow?

IRAKO SEIHAKU (1877-1946)

Wandering
(from *The Peacock Boat*)

Autumn wind flaps the thin straw curtain
hung in the doorway.
The river inn is a crown of loneliness.

The lonely traveller
sings in a soft, deep voice
while he looks at the sky.

He envisions his dead mother as a young girl.
Her white brow
appears in the moon.

His dead father, reborn as a child,

moves his round shoulders
across the Milky Way.

Light filters white across the river
through the willows.
From Ono on the other bank
a flute makes its faint way through mist,
touching the traveller's heart.

He sighs what he can of a plaintive song
learned in the vale where he was born.
The deep, absorbing melody
ricochets off the flute in the sky
and the wind that groans
out of the earth's bowels.

His mother is at rest in his heart
and his father has become a boy again.
The flute from Ono
wafts a faint
melody
in the mist.

He goes on singing,
smiling,
as though
a boy again.

Seihaku's poem is established as a masterpiece. In spite of its mere eighteen
poems, *The Peacock Boat* will ensure Seihaku's fame for as long as there is a
literature. Separated from his parents while still young, he was raised as a
wanderer; the traveller of this poem is perhaps an alter ego. The dedication to
The Peacock Boat reads: "For the soul of my Mother, who Sleeps in the Bosom
of her Hometown Deep in the Mountains." Because his father was still alive
when the poem was first published, the poem's traveler is not exactly the same
person as Seihaku.

As for the lonely river inn with its thin straw curtain, we are seized not merely
by chilly desolation. In a lonely, low voice a traveller reared in a remote
hometown in the mountains begins to sing in almost a melodic groan that seems
to rise from the depths of the earth. In his vision his dead mother is transformed

into a maiden whose white forehead seems to appear in the moon; and the apparition of his dead father as a young boy moves round-shouldered across the Milky Way.

The soft sounds of the flute from Ono on the opposite bank ricochet across the misty sky. The tentative, plaintive traveller's song is shot through with echoes. At last, his mother and father revived in his mind, he smiles, forgetting his loneliness as he returns to his childhood. The image that emerges is exact on account of the plain, repetitive five-seven-five syllabic rhythm. The traveller's sorrow, his longing for his parents and his nostalgia for his hometown are all blended in a strangely vivid way.

KITAHARA HAKUSHŪ

The Larch
(from *Poems in India Ink*)

I

Passing through
a grove of larches
I looked carefully and thought,
'A traveller encounters such solitude!'

II

And I went into still another grove
and followed along
a narrow path
that led on and on.

III

Deep into the recesses of this grove
I followed along the path
misted with rain
and swept by a mountain wind.

IV

I was absolutely alone
on a narrow path,
a path so desolate
no one would tarry.

V

Coming out of the grove
I stopped, for no reason,
and thought how lonely the larches.
I whispered, 'Larches.'

VI

Coming out
I saw the mist atop Mt. Asama,
a mist rising above it,
a mist over the larches.

VII

Rain clarifies the shapes of everything,
bringing clarity to the loneliness.
A single cuckoo cries.
The larches are drenched in rain and mist.

VIII

World, you are a lonely world.
Though you are not eternal I feel glad.
The river speaks among the mountains;
the wind speaks among the larches.

In August 1921 when Hakushū had gone to lecture at a summer school in Hoshino Hot Springs (in the Shinshū District), he got the idea for this poem. The major spas in that area are Karuizawa, Kutsukake, and Oiwake. The Hoshino spa is near Kutsukake and so the larch groves would have been near there or near Oiwake.

Beautiful highland trees such as larches, firs, silver firs and birches rarely appear in poems before the Meiji Era. It is odd that Japanese poets, notable for their sensitivity to the changing seasons, had been so neglectful. It may be that the Japanese esthetic is such that they missed the trees for the forest. Around the beginning of the Meiji period, European and American missionaries regularly found relief in the cool places of the highlands such as Karuizawa and Kamikochi, and from that time on, perhaps, the Japanese began to open their eyes to the beauty of the larches and birches. Behind this development, too, lay Futabatei Shimei's *Rendezvous* (a virtual translation of Turgenev's *A Sportsman's Sketches*) and—a book influenced by *Rendezvous*—Kunikida Doppo's description of a copse in his *Musashino*.

At the time Hakushū was enchanted by things fragile, subtle and profound. He liked the somehow lonely aspect of a larch's look, in which respect it resembled a traveller. As he plodded along a lonely path through the larch trees he sensed that the world was a lonely place. His annotation of this poem reads:

> The subtle and profound in a larch and the lonesome and faint in the wind should be passed on from heart to heart and I realized that the whisper in the winds is a whisper in my heart. Dear readers, rather than read or sing this poem aloud, appreciate it in silence with its sounds and scents.

SHAKU CHŌKŪ (1887-1953)

Stone Stupas
(from *Between Seas and Mountains*)

(The newly-erected Horse-head Crown Kannon stands off by itself as one of many stone monuments commemorating horses. The graves of travelers mark every mountain pass and some of those were fatally ill persons who dared take this last journey without informing their families of their illness.)

> Their time is past,
> yet
> men and horses indeed died
> and some died from fatigue
> on their journey.
>
> Horses
> died on the path.
> Ah,

the journey
is unending.

Down in the undergrowth
of a pine grove
on this lonely mountain,
sunlight secretly visits
a traveler's stupa.

In the secret silence
of their hearts
they in their last moments
could find
nothing to say.

All the dead
along the path
leave graves,
plain, obscure,
and grassy.

Hakushū's essay, "A Traveller in Black", is subtitled, "On Origuchi's Tanka" (Chōkū's real name, the poet himself having been, as well, a scholar of Japanese literature). In it, Hakushū writes:

Compared to certain *Man'yōshū* poets, [Chōkū] more closely resembles Kurohito than Hitomaro. As far as the contemplation of nature is concerned, Chōkū finds Kurohito deeper than Akahito; Chōkū's work is subtle and complex. He uses Kurohito as a starting point and yet embarks upon an apparently endless journey. We can barely hear him breathe as he crosses mountains and rivers in his phantom-like progress. Dust swirls on the path in front of him, filling his eyes, even in the absence of sound and wind.

"A Traveller in Black" suits Chōkū to a tee. The most striking, the most touching of all his many subjects is that of travelling. In order to collect folklore he was accustomed to visiting isolated islands and other out-of-the-way places; he deliberately trod the deserted mountain path, slept on a bed of grass and tossed his hat over windmills, which amazed his travelling mentor Yanagida Kunio.

The five tanka above are based on his travels in July 1920 through Nakatsugawa in Minō (now the southern area of Gifu Prefecture), visiting mountain villages around the Shinano-Tōtoumi-Mikawa border. Such celebrations as the Snow Festival, the Flower Festival, and others, were still important in those days. Having heard from Hayakawa Kōtarō about these festivals, Chōkū set off at once to see them. In annotating his own tanka, he writes:

> On many paths among the mountains or along the sea I saw many stupas, old and new, of those who died on their journeys. In other cases, a fallen horse was commemorated with a stupa crowned by a horse's head. This goddess Kannon testifies to the fact that people have worshipped men and animals that abruptly disappeared from the world. I constantly in my travels run across such stupas. My sorrow is constantly renewed as though the dead were being awakened.

Chōkū as a traveller here confesses that he is deeply moved by men and horses that fell by the wayside. People used to recite the first tanka citing "men and horses" as one of their favorites. The Japanese original uses not the active but the passive form of the verb, thus stressing the interpenetration of pilgrims and their deaths as an endless process. The figures of long dead and anonymous travellers and horses loom up in Chōkū's mind.

The following waka of Takechi-no-Kurohito in the *Man'yōshū* impressed Chōkū greatly:

> The little boat
> that sailed around Cape Are—
> where will it find shelter?
> Ah,
> that helpless little boat.

 Half-way up a mountain,
In the midst of my journey
I feel homesick

and see far out at sea
a vermilion ship.

We will dock
at the port in Hira.
Don't row too far away
from shore.
It is night; it is late.

If I am encompassed
by the darkness of night
on the marshy plains of Kachino
in Takashima,
where—how—can I sleep?

These four waka reflect the loneliness, the desolation, that the author felt on his journey. The boat he is observing fills him with a sense of loneliness as he ponders its passengers'—and his own—isolation. The other traveller, though a complete stranger, now becomes, as night falls, an object of pity. The feeling is universal.

Chōkū hoped himself to develop the sensitivity, empathy and purity shown by Kurohito. In Chōkū's tanka given below we can see that he has succeeded:

(from "An Island Mountain")

The arrowroot blossoms,
having been trampled on,
are giving off new colors.
Some wayfarers must have walked
this mountain path.

(from "Back Pain Mountain")

Travellers passing along the path
leave their loneliness behind.
The man who passed me around Ōno
is now no more
than a mere dot.

(from "A Path that Faces the Rocks")

I wonder
if the child who wandered
along the lonely Nima shore
has reached
home.

(from "The Mountain from One Year to Another")

Voices on the mountain
are bass and occasional.
As night came on in Kiso
a few deer and I
walked along the ridge.

Travelling provides an opportunity to feel the loneliness of fellow-travellers. In the vastness of existence the self and other selves encounter one another as separate entities. The famous "arrowroot blossoms" tanka is based on the deep murmur of a lonesome traveller. His sentiment traces back to a consciousness of solidarity with unknown persons who had walked on the same mountain path long ago. He speaks of others but he is the traveller and his words will return to him. The solidarity is between the passing and the passed.

All Chōkū's tanka given here ostensibly were based upon his journey to Iki Island but in fact were a product of his journey to Kumano. Journeys past and present overlap.

MURŌ SAISEI

Lonely Spring
(from *Collected Lyric Poems*)

Sunlight drips incessantly.
A waterwheel revolves in melancholy.
I can see the mountains in Echigo
against the blue.
How lonely I feel.

Speechless all day,
I walk along the field
And see rape blossoms
waving in the distance.
This is the pinnacle
of loneliness.

One day in February 1914 Saisei visited Hagiwara Sakutarō in Maebashi. He stayed until 8th March in an inn by the Tone River. They had learned of each other in the poetry journal *Zamboa*, edited by Kitahara Hakushū. Sakutarō initiated the meeting in a letter to Saisei; their friendship lasted a lifetime.

At this time in 1914, in Tokyo, Saisei was impoverished and ran away to Maebashi on a one-way ticket.

In spite of the cold in Maebashi from late February into early March, sunlight glowed as brilliantly as spring itself; the waterwheel turned slowly in a lonely stream, and far off on the Jōetsu border the mountains stood in sharp relief. In those days when spring was in the offing the lonely traveller could not shake off his loneliness, which was the common adolescent phenomenon of melancholy. Sun and dancing field flowers deepened his loneliness. Ōtomo-no-Yakamochi's waka in the *Man'yōshū* reads:

A skylark soars
in soft sunlight.
Alone on my horse,
I am helpless to shake off
my melancholy.

The resemblance of Saisei's poem to this waka is obvious.

154

SATŌ HARUO

Song of a Traveller around Cape Inubō
(from *The Poems of Satō Haruo*)

I'm here to pluck
an unknown flower,
as a maiden might.
Walking on my own shadow,
I cannot tell the height of a lighthouse
unless I look up at it.
The surging waves are no match
for those of my hometown.
I think that the pines
growing on the deserted strand
are rusty-black;
and
so is my heart.

One of Haruo's earlier poems, he deliberately entitled it in allusion to Tōson's "Song of a Traveller along the Chikuma River." Whereas Tōson's poem is made of melancholic lyricism, backed by a nostalgia for times past, Haruo's is purely ironic, as already seen in the first three lines. His mind, far from maidenly, has rusted. The air and the sky above the deserted strand are chilly; the waves of Haruo's town—Kishū—are emerald blue; these are not. The expected feelings one develops on a journey are here inverted.

WAKAYAMA BOKUSUI

[Two tanka composed in the Chūgoku District]
(from *The Voice of the Sea*)

Today, again,
I go on walking,
longing,
tolling a bell over and over
in my mind.

On this journey
how many mountains
and rivers must I cross
to reach
a land of no sorrows?

(nine tanka from *On the Road*)

—Written while hiking around Mt.Asama in Shinano, early September to mid-November—

Tired of gathering walnuts,
I lay down
on the grass.
Dragonflies came
and talked to me.

Some roadside flowers
speak the truth:
perishable things
are really
precious.

White teeth
pierced by hot autumn sake:
ah, nothing can surpass
the joy of drinking alone,
silently.

From the second story
of a doctor's house
in Komoro
the view of Mt. Asama
is stunning.

Behind an old station
at the foot of the mountain

there is a darkish,
running stream
whose banks I love.

While I cross Mt. Asama,
wisps of smoke
rise
toward the pale,
passing clouds.

The scuffling
of a brown-backed
baby lizard
among autumn leaves
is pure loneliness.

Suddenly
in the dead of winter
I emerge from my daze
and find myself
walking across the grassy mountain.

After a bath
I sit alone
and catch the loneliness
of this journey
rising from my skin.

Among those poets who believe life to be a journey, Bashō stands between his predecessor Saigyō and the modern poet Bokusui. The major topics in Bokusui's tanka were travelling, sake and love.

Everybody agreed that among the tanka poets whose hearts sang most eagerly and melodiously, Bokusui and Yoshii Isamu led the way. They neither stumbled nor hesitated in singing their songs. Bokusui's work was unaffectedly simple, direct and lyrical.

Some of our most cherished tanka were composed by Takuboku and Bokusui; particularly loved, among Bokusui's, is the one above that begins, "On this journey...." It is universally known in Japan. The urge to travel is a formless longing with the anticipation of nothing in return, the more so when the urge is that and nothing more. Travelling is life; the height of loneliness; and a positive way to deal with desolateness.

YOSHII ISAMU

A Ravine in Nirau

In November 1934 in a ravine in Inono Village, Nirau, the Tosa District, I built myself a hermit's thatched hut and called it "Keiki-so" [lit. "devil's torrent hut']. In this hermitage I shut myself up.

Being lonely,
I grow intimate
with clouds,
which are of course
not human.

Being lonely,
I recall only
my past life
of luxury
and elegance.

Being lonely,
I feel nostalgic
when I see a patch
of snow that remains
on Mt. Gozaisho's side.

Being lonely,
I open the sliding door
before dawn
and find deep frost
spread across Inono Village.

Being lonely,
I brought from deep in the mountains
a rock and set it in my garden.
I sit on it
like an enlightened monk.

Being lonely,
I hear
from the mountain
in pitch darkness
a fox's barking.

Being lonely,
I think I shall hear nothing
of the lawsuit in Naniwa.
Nor should I
have expected to.

Being lonely,
I look through a book
on the topography of Tosa
and recall certain rocks
at Cape Kanawa.

Being lonely—
this ravine in Nirau
utterly snowed-in—
I heat sake at the hearth
to revive my spirits.

Being lonely,
I arrange winter chrysanthemums
in a bamboo basket
so as to refresh
my memory of her.

Being lonely,
I hear
in the wind-blown shoji
the rustling
of her kimono.

Being lonely,
I suddenly seem to smell
a lacquered image of Buddha.
I look restlessly
about the room.

Isamu divorced in November 1933 because the newspapers had picked up his wife's activities and scandalized him. He resigned his title and aristocratic rank, and determined to live as a hermit in Tosa. Earlier, in August, he had gone through the Keihan District (Kyoto and Osaka) en route to Tosa, where he stayed for about three months (in Inono Village). By September, however, he had already decided to remain in Inono Village.

In Nirau Ravine
in Tosa
my hermitage
should be ensconced
deeply, and deeper.

For supper
at a mountain inn
in Inono Village
I boil knotweed
to go with my sake.

It's only natural.
It was all my fault.
So I will hide
deep in the mountains
of Tosa.

He wrote these tanka, then, in the fall of 1933. He built his hermitage in November, thus commencing his lonely life.

His life now closely resembled the lives of medieval hermits. More than all others, Isamu resembled Saigyo, the medieval hermit, although Saigyo's voice reflects the tone of an even more severe isolation.

Abadoning his family and the estate, he entered upon a life not unlike that of a priest. Poet-priests who go to that extreme are rare these days. In this tanka series when he is immersed in extreme loneliness, he yet seems carefree; nonetheless, the pervasive tone of his lines is one of the deep loneliness of human existence.

Apart from his actual circumstances in these years, we find that his exquisite tanka fill us with admiration.

NAKANO SHIGEHARU

Whitecaps
(from *The Poems of Nakano Shigeharu*)

Long, narrow and deserted, this strand.
Surges far out build and gather
and attack the shore;
waves climb, and collapsing in autumnal forms,
cry their loneliness out
upon these sands.
They cry out of the depths, the cry resounding
against the close and hard cliffs.
Between cliff and sea a tough little train struggles on,
its windows twined by a misty spray.
Ah, Echigo and you shores of Oyashirazu and Ichifuri!
As the breakers swell and crash
this traveller's mind feels splashed and chill.

Shigeharu recounts his train passage along what used to be known as one of the most perilous spots in the Hokuriku District. Bashō, in *The Narrow Road to the Deep North*, writes:

Today we walked through the most dangerous of all places
in this north country. The very names tell all: 'Oblivious of

Parents,' 'Oblivious of Children,' 'Dogs Turn Back' and 'Turn
Your Horses Back.' Exhausted, we went to bed early.

And in that travelogue he inserted a haiku in which he records his having seen
a courtesan in an inn in Ichifuri.

Oyashirazu, where the mountain rises steeply from the beach, affords a path
so dangerous, the waves unrelenting, that either children or parents who take
that path can be said to be oblivious of each other (i.e., not to care about the
others' feelings). Shigeharu has been deeply impressed by the whitecaps
constantly breaking against the mountain, which has been gradually eroded
along this "Long, narrow and deserted" beach. He beautifully depicts the
whitecaps that cry out their "loneliness" and break in "autumnal forms." How
aptly "autumnal forms" echoes the sense of desolation.

He does not avoid the names of those chilly, lonely, dark places along the
Japan Sea—obviously, "Oblivious of Parents," "Oblivious of Children" and
other such names underscore the grimness of the landscape. Aboard the
slow-moving train his traveller's heart "feels splashed and chill." Because he
does not explicitly solicit our pity, the lines all the more plumb emotional
depths, and thus we should term this one of those poems in which word and
intention are perfectly matched.

MIYOSHI TATSUJI

The Cape in Spring
(from *The Surveying Ship*)

Gliding above the cape in spring at journey's end, a seagull;

in the distance, undulating on the horizon, the sea.

This is the first poem in the collection and similar to a tanka. According to
accounts he wrote it while boating from Shimoda to Numazu. He had been to
Izu Yugashima to call on his friend Kajii Motojiro in hospital. He may have
suddenly seen Cape Irozaki as he sailed and thus conceived the poem.

Another poem of his—a prose poem—called "The Mountain Pass," though
composed in autumn, he wrote when he went from Yugashima through the
Amagi Pass to Shimoda. In it the following passsage occurs and may be seen
as somewhat explanatory of "The Cape in Spring".

.....Days and days lie behind me on the path. The sorrow of
the traveller's heart grows upon me like an illness, yet what I
feel must be none other than the feeling the ancients had who,
singing of the passing seasons, attached their hearts to nature.
The sea will soon come into view; but now, this autumn, my
heart is sore!

Ah, I shall listen to the wind-swept pines in the seashore
village, steep myself in the hot bath of a dimly-lit inn and
look out the window at the cape before darkness falls—I
heard waves lap at my heart as I walked along the pass.

"At journey's end" (from "The Cape in Spring") actually means the end of many
nights spent on the road; weary of body and heart, sorrow engulfs him "like an
illness." In the context of that sorrow the Cape and the seagull arise like an
image of light in a picture he is looking at at the journey's conclusion. As the
boat moves away, the landscape of his mind slowly fades and he is left with
poignant sorrow.

Kusasenrihama

(from *Kusasenri*)

I walked this district years ago;
stood at dawn on a mountain top—
great Mt. Aso in the Higa District.
Grass covers the lower slopes
of this unchanging, majestic, smoking figure.
The summit is veiled today
in nostalgic indigo.
The view is as in a dream.
But oh,
where have my youthful hopes gone,
the interval of twenty-years,
my friends and unrequited love?
They deserted me.
As spring passes on this overcast day
I've grown older
and yet have come to visit once more.
I lean on my rude cane
and peer in all directions:

Great Mt. Aso set in Hi-no-kuni!
Horses romping on the high meadow.
Such loneliness in the name: Kusasenrihama

The first line reminds us of Tatsuji's having previously hiked to Kusasenrihama (as recorded in the earlier poem "Great Mt. Aso"). He then goes on to recall his youthful hopes, the lapse of twenty years, old friends and former loves, all of which he contrasts with the unchanging mountain, green grass and other aspects of nature's permanence. "Where is the self of yesterday?" he asks, feeling bereft and indeed feeling quite old under the lowering clouds on this languid day. In fact he was still in his early forties. He stands alone with his walking stick after a tiring journey.

Exaggerating, he tries to pass himself off as an old man; but then he may well do so, his ideas of course being entirely subjective. This poet in his wandering may have felt age setting in earlier than others would feel it. The base of his outlook is two-fold: mutability and swift passage.

Thus, as in a kaleidoscope, various memories wink and are gone. They resemble transient daydreams on a cloudy day in the progress of spring. He rehearses his fond memories with great satisfaction where now, a solitary soul, he stands on an immense meadow in Kusasenrihama on a vast plateau. One recalls Saigyō's waka:

Aging, withal,
this may be
the last time in my life
that I shall cross
the Nakayama Pass in Saya.

Tatsuji's state of mind, like Saigyō's, is steeped in a modern melancholy pertinent to his time and place.

A Song of Korea
(from *A Single Bell*)

The imperial mausoleum of a king of Silla
on a day of serenity in autumn—how lonely.

From afar comes the crowing of a cock
and the sound of a shuttle as a farmer's wife weaves a kimono.

I am a traveller from a distant place.
Let me rest here a while on the still green grass.

In the fields white cotton flowers shine
and hidden crickets chirp in the lanes.

Wind idles through the tops of pines.
I see a brook as I elbow through the grass.

I look languidly here and there
and hear the random sounds of shuttles.

A moment of stillness is interrupted
by a bee come dancing down from heaven.

The stone lion cowers in the heat of the sun
and stone figures crouch when I bow in respect.

One day the dead will return to this spot—
kings, queens, all the people, and roads and palaces, too.

Is this an illusion, this girl dancing in her gossamer cloth
as light as a dream? Or is it a mere cloud flying over the woods?

I cut a pathway through the grass and turn to look at the palace ruins.
Ancient beads of dew glisten to both sides of the path.

Straight necked, tail down, a big cow
stands still, a transparent shadow.

Blue sky
and burial mounds....

Truth to say, the past altogether
lies hidden in the earth.

A magpie strolls
in silence.

The grass blades have ears.
They listen to autumn wind.

Tatsuji walked through several parts of Korea during a trip in September 1940. Silla was one of several separate parts of what is now known as Korea. The capital of the southeastern region was called Ch'ing Chou and is the grave site of Wu Lieh, the twenty-ninth king. In a convention of waka, "takubusuma" (an epithet for "Silla") indicates bedding made of white mulberry wood and so the word always signifies whiteness.

After paying respect to the king's mausoleum in Silla, Tatsuji walked along looking about at the rare white cotton flowers. Crickets in the lane, wind in the pines and the murmur of a stream filled his ears. Stone lions and male figures lined both sides of the walk leading to the mausoleum. The royal mausoleum said in effect that "history lies buried here." A lone magpie walked in the wind-blown grass.

The poet's retrospective heart sensitively recreated things Korean in all the lyricism of a vast continental spectacle.

Though the setting and the atmosphere are different, the poem reminds us of Tōson's "At an Old Castle in Komoro."

HAGIWARA SAKUTARŌ

On a Journey
(from *Pure Lyrical Pieces*)

I'd like to go to France
but it's too far,
so I buy a new suit
and set out for anywhere.
As the train passes along the mountain
I lean against the azure window
and think of delightful things.
A morning in May at dawn,
and my heart is like a young herb growing willy-nilly.

It's not as if he did not say he wanted to go to France. We must understand the poem's irony. For most Japanese literary and artistic persons France for long had been a desirable place to go, but here he pretends in jest that "too far" is just "too far."

What he is suggesting instead is that we—he, readers, others—should set out to explore Japan with no particular destination in mind. In such lines as "I lean against the azure window/and think of delightful things" he is imagining himself altogether free from restraints. This poem, among his "Passionate Love Poems" in *Pure Lyrical Pieces*, was written before his *Howling at the Moon* collection.

A Song of a Wanderer
(from *Ice Island*)

The sun rises above a precipice
and melancholy stoops low under a footbridge.
The sky is immeasurably distant.
A lonely shadow drifts behind the fence
along the endless railroad track.

Ah, you wanderer,
you come out of the past and go beyond the future,
you who seek eternal nostalgia;
how palely, how painfully—
how clocklike—you loiter.
You should break the circle of self-indulgence,
kill it
as you would a snake with a rock.

Huh....you're lonelier than a devil.
You've withstood the frosty winter.
Having never believed anything,
you've felt angry at what you believe in.
You blame yourself for lust
and yet without true reason.
Weary, depressed, how can you return
to the one who will tenderly embrace and kiss you?—
you who've never loved anything
and never been loved.

You poor wretch!
You drift sadly, idly in the setting sun,
around a precipice,
your hometown truly nowhere,
your hometown truly nowhere.

In the preface to *Ice Island* Sakutarō writes:

> My life so far has been like a man drifting on a desolate
> iceberg in the polar regions of the North Sea. I felt enisled
> on a berg from where I could see the phantasmal aurora
> borealis; I yearned, felt distressed, by turns elated, saddened
> and benighted, and grew angry at myself as I drifted along
> vainly with the flow. I am the Eternal Wanderer, homeless.
> The sky above my heart is the invariably dismal one of the
> polar region. The fierce wind roars and tears my soul apart.
> I hope to have recorded in these poems the pain of my
> life—as a kind of diary of my life.

The Eternal Wanderer, in other words, is a desolate person, this being the
subject of "A Song of a Wanderer". Sakutarō added a prefatory note to the
poem in which he states that "A man who walks under a footbridge along the
precipice—that in essence is I: the shadow of the figure of the wanderer" in a
climate of abject desolation and nothingness, walking alone, forever. This in a
nutshell is Sakutarō as traveller. Cut off from nostalgia ("eternal nostalgia"),
because having no hometown to return to, he walks along the precipice of life
in unqualified isolation.

NISHIWAKI JUNZABURŌ (1894-1982)

No Traveller Returns
(from *No Traveller Returns*)

Traveller, you must wait
before you bathe your tongue
in this trickling spring.
Traveller of life, you must think yourself also
nothing but a water spirit

oozing from a crevice in a rock.
This thinking water does not run on forever.
It will peter out before it reaches eternity.
How raucous the jay!
A phantom with a flower
sometimes emerges from this water.
The search for eternal life is illusory.
Sending desire into the flowing stream
and finally
falling off the precipice,
wishing to disappear, is not folly.
Those words come from this water imp
who also flows along to emerge playfully from the water
       in the village and town
when water weeds rise beneath reflected clouds.

Sakutarō's "Song of a Wanderer" can be heard in this poem. The crucial difference is, however, Junzaburō's cool-headedness throughout and his wit, including humor. By contrast, Sakutarō's voice is loud with anger. "These poems," Sakutarō writes, "are for oral presentaion and are written with that in mind. They should only be read aloud. They are for singing." (Preface to *Ice Island*). Junzaburō's poem, on the other hand, demands to be read in private and in silence.

   In the Preface to *No Traveller Returns* Junzaburō's writes:

> ......Various characters are hidden inside me. First a modern man and an ancient man are both present, the former represented by modern science, philosophy, theology and literature, and the latter by primitive culture, psychology and folklore.
>
> Still one other man remains who is unsure whether he represents the mystery of life or that of eternity in space. This man whom I call the" Phantom Figure" I regard as an eternal traveller. He comes and goes at will; it may be the remnant in our subconsciousness of primeval experience which causes him thus to appear.
>
> The word "eternal" means to me the unavoidable acceptance of nothingness (extinction) rather than its denial. Looking at a blade of grass in the process of sprouting

arouses in me something like 'eternal memories', which mischief I attribute to the 'Phantom Figure.'

Unlike the eternal wanderer, who is Sakutarō himself, the Phantom Figure serves as the author's alter ego. It appears in other sections of *No Traveller Returns* in such phrases as "The Phantom Figure exudes sadness", "The Phantom Figure is lonely" and "The Phantom Figure departs." In his poems Junzaburō's sets the Phantom Figure walking along in some place such as the Musashino Plain and has him stooping to touch the red bud of a spear flower, an acorn and the dead leaves of the zelkova tree. He reminds us of the "eternal memory" which is "the radical loneliness of being" carried even in trifling objects.

Junzaburō himself, while in reality strolling along the Musashino Plain, is in continual quest of something, because in his mind the "Phantom Figure" really exists. What he keenly feels is nothing less than profound human loneliness. His idea of poetry is clearly refelected in the following poem (No.39) from *No Traveller Returns*:

I can no longer write a poem.
Where no poem is, a poem is.
Only bits of reality can constitute poems.
Reality is a loneliness.
I am; therefore, I feel lonely.
Loneliness is the essence of existence
and beauty basically tends toward loneliness.
Beauty is the symbol of eternity.

The "Phantom Figure" or the "Eternal Traveller" is loneliness proper, this being the core of Junzaburō's poetics. "Loneliness" in *No Traveller Returns* abounds:

-2-

A dim light
shines through the window.
The human world is loneliness.

170

-7-

A man puts his head out the window.
Gentians grow in his garden.
His wife frowns in thought.
This man who lives
in a corner of the lane
where zelkova leaves are falling—
this man is loneliness itself.

-45-

Loneliness is an open window.

-46-

When autumn comes
I recall those early years
strolling the Musashino Plain:
I heard my own tomorrow in the crackling
 rustic yellow leaves I trod on.
I gathered a few oak leaves
and set them on my desk
and for quite a while
regarded the plain.
The reddish buds on the bare branches
seemed to be shrivelling.
Spring had gone down deep into winter
and loneliness was the buds on those branches.

-54-

I sit in the light of a paper lantern
in an inn. It is autumn
and valerian is blooming.
Cricket song is steeped in stillness.
I begin to read a letter.
Loneliness is the field.

-72-

Having read in a priest's book
great praise of the laurel tree
I went looking for it
on the Musashino Plains
but found nothing.
Then next to the outdoor toilet of a school
I ran into a single ragged, crooked laurel.
Loneliness is in oddity.

-78-

At summer's end, at Koma Station
I bought a pear from an old peasant.
She gestured oddly,
to make me laugh
and to express her thanks.
And I wished a folklorist had seen that.
Loneliness is in remnants of myth.

Poems of this sort inevitably remind us of waka in the time of the
Shin-Kokinshū in which life's loneliness is typically located in autumnal images.
The essence of an autumn evening is sought for in poems that produce a nearly
unimaginable sense of loneliness. For instance, these three waka:

Colors don't produce loneliness.
There are countless evergreens
here in the mountains.
And, autumn evening,
you surely feel loneliness.
(Jakuren)

Though I abandoned worldly desires
I could not but feel pity
when I saw a single sandpiper

standing as in prayer
on this darkening autumn marsh.
(Saigyo)

Wandering around this deserted sea coast
I found
no flowers, no brilliant maples,
but a simple tea hut
and autumn evening.
(Teika)

These are the three superlative waka on "autumn evening" found in the
Shin-Kokinshū.

KIYAMA SHŌHEI

A Traveller's Song
(from *The Poems of Kiyama Shōhei*)

When the man turned sixty
he entrained around a bay
formed by a volcanic eruption.
Even in May
with plum and cherry blossoming
a cold rain had slipped into sleet.

As the train passed through a station on the bluff
I saw the rusty inclined roofs of fishermen's houses.
From an eave some private red garment had been
hung out to dry. She must have been born in 1904!
She'd been married forty years.
The red was gray-red, like a leaf in the marsh.

The houses gave on to the sea,
the rear on to the tracks.
This was called existence.
The man's train, bound for Abashiri,
was detouring around the bay in the rain.

This poem seems to epitomize Shōhei's fiction. The thrust is a sort of wind-borne wanderlust. It was published in 1966 when he was in his sixties. Though it was May a sleety rain was falling as he passed through a forlorn fishing village. He saw a red object hanging from the eave. This sort of humorous image, unique in Shōhei's work, inclines the reader to smile—but he doesn't, because the poet's mien is more serious than ever. The garment, he claims, not only belonged to an old woman, but one who was born in 1904. That would make her his age; she and he would have endured the same decades and thus he felt sympathy for her, as for a wife. His verbal brush work is realistic: she is a gray-red leaf fallen at life's end into the marsh.

The red garment as the conspicuous focus of the image all the more arouses the sense of the journey's loneliness. The fishermen's houses face the sea; the backs, the train tracks. The very line "This was called existence." enables the poet to abstract from the individual to the universal. All human beings are encompassed. It is Shōhei's wit that keeps the pity under control.

TANAKA FUYUJI (1894-1980)

In the Hokuriku District
(from *On a Late Spring Day*)

Every name along the Hokuriku Line
has a lonely sound: Nō, Kajiyashiki, Itoigawa,
Ōmi, Oyashirazu, Ichiburi, Tomari, Nyūzen....
Nō spreads along the coast and smells of fish.
The cracks in the floor of a fish shop
frame the blue sea like a movie screen.
White gulls sail just over the waves.
An old wood-roofed inn stands alone,
its seaside shutters half-closed by day,
a day somewhat warm like tepid gelatin,
as a blind masseur whistles along the road.
Every name has a lonely sound:
Nō, Kajiyashiki, Itoigawa,
Ōmi, Oyashirazu, Ichiburi, Tomari, Nyūzen....

The poet wants to isolate pure desolation on this journey to the Hokuriku District. Station names educe a sense of loneliness; the description of the town of Nō is particularly detailed in its seaside loneliness, the shutters of the inn half-shut on the sea. One wonders if Fuyuji slept there. When we observe the decaying atmosphere, as the blind masseur whistles along, we are plunged into the depth of loneliness.

In another poem—"Spring"—Fuyuji enumerates the same place names and states that "Whereas this Pacific night is moonlit and misty/a violent snowstorm rages on the Sea of Japan." Fuyuji intones the essential loneliness of human beings as he ponders the desolateness of towns in the district. This poet experienced various branch transfers in line with his long employment by a bank. In each locale he would have experienced what ordinary Japanese life is and learned to cherish it while at the same time understanding its difficulties.

VIII

Hometown Memories

KITAHARA HAKUSHŪ

Prologue
(from *Memories*)

Are memories not like
the probing antennae
of a red-banded firefly
wafting phosphorescence in the afternoon?

Or are they some indistinct rare grain flower
or a reaper's singing of a ballad
or the soft white glow of a dove's feathers picked
in the warm clime of a wine cellar?

If memories be sounds they are flutes;
or a harmonica played in twilight
when the toads are croaking;
or the familiar medicine prescribed by a family doctor.

If memories be scents, they are of velvet,
the queen's eyes in a pack of cards
and the melancholic mien
of a jesting pierrot.

Memories do not glow with
the bright pain of fever.
They are after all as soft as late spring—
are they not my autumn legends?

This is the prologue to Hakushū's second poetry collection, *Memories* (June 1911). He depicts boyhood memories in his hometown of Yanagawa and these are exclusively sensuous memories. A kaleidoscope of sensuousness is developed, all the images consisting of metaphors.

First of all metaphors are "the probing antennae of a red-banded firefly" in the afternoon. It seems probable that Hakushū's lines are recalling Bashō:

It struck me that
in daytime
a firefly's neck is red indeed.

Then, too, the riverine area of Yanagawa is inseparable from the image of fireflies. In an essay Hakushū states:

> ...when this riotous merry-making has subsided, the firefly season will come again to Yanagawa:
>
>> Are those dazzling eyes the eyes of
>> stars, fireflies or cormorants?
>> If fireflies, alight on my hand.
>> If stars, I'll make a wish....
>
> Such nursery rhymes as this were often sung to me when I was a baby. Strapped to my nurse's back and scared of the dark, I gingerly reached out, and when I took hold of a firefly my heart, filled with curiosity, trembled. Actually, the firefly is a renowned presence in this locality. When white potato flowers are in bloom, small boats go up the Yabe River in succession. In season, all the boatmen cage the fireflies, that turn their phosphorescent breath off and on, and float down stream in the darkness with the dream-like piercing paleness of their tiny passengers.

In another poem—"Canals"—the voice of the firefly ("whoo-whoo") is heard across the canals of Yanagawa. But to return to "Prologue," "the warm clime of a wine cellar" probably refers to one of the Kitahara wineries, a historic old firm called "Aburaya" or "Futsudoiya." The canal reflected the store's exterior white plaster walls.

That Hakushū enjoyed a relatively exotic boyhood is suggested by such words as "velvet," "the queen's eyes" and "pierrot." The soft velvet touch doubtless alludes to both the sentiment of his memories and the odor of exoticism.

Although memories are often accompanied by pain, his poem does not suggest pain or a high fever; instead, we feel the soft touch of late spring or the sweet taste of Gothic legends that he read on autumn days.

The poem is utterly shot through with metaphors that do, however, attach to his memories.

Yanagawa
(from *Memories*)

And here we have Yanagawa,
Yanagawa!
Look at that copper torii.
And the parapet along that bridge.
(The coachman stops blowing his horn
and shades his eyes against the fierce sun.)

Thistles throng the front of the house.
The house....
The house
was once a brothel,
now an old deserted brothel.

The girl sitting on the *banco*
is my neighbor's stepdaughter.
Stepdaughter.
That reflection on the water—
in the reflection she is winding
a small rubber ball that was her mother's—
winding that small ball with red wool,
crying,
her hands wet with tears.

And listen to that, traveller.
Traveller,
hear that samisen?
Look at that grebe bobbing out there.
(The coachman blows his horn
and enters the town at sunset.)

Sunset, sunrise,
Dawn clear tomorrow.

The scene of course is Yanagawa sketched in the manner of a ball-bouncing song—light and bright. Nosukai, the name of the old brothel, is a dialectic word for prostitute and *banco* is a Japanese corruption of the Portuguese for "veranda."

(from "My Early Life")

My hometown of Yanagawa contains many riverine canals.It is a quiet, decaying town. Nature in all respects there is typically tropical. Among the odors carried on the canals is that of the continuously decaying white plaster walls of feudal times, now reflected on the water.clear water flows into the decaying town...under the forlorn kitchen of Nosukaiya...running through the bleached cotton in the hands of a washer-woman...dammed up by a lockgate...lamenting over the black dahlias in front of a small café while the sporadic sounds of a samisen are wafted in the afternoon air...water used to make sake...water that moistens the lips of a consumptive girl, her skin shiny after a bath, where she stands drawing water...water troubled by the feathers of a timid duck...and at night when the dear old lanterns lit for the reading of the Kannon sutra are flickering, water flows down the Shio River toward the sea's edge which I can see just below the rain gutter of my house. Thus these numerous quiet canals are reflected, as they have always been, as lonely as bright shadows on the white walls.... Canals that served as waterways to theater and eased the passage of snakes and kept the secrets of a young, adventurous boy. The canal town of Yanagawa is a gray water coffin.

There is no better commentary on Hakushū's poem than this.

MURŌ SAISEI

A Strange Landscape (II)
(from *Collected Lyric Poems*)

Hometowns should be thought of from afar,
while singing a sad tune.
Even if one should be down and out
and reduced to begging in a foreign land,
one should never return.
Alone in this town at twilight,
I never think of my hometown without growing teary.
Taking these words to heart,
I shall go back that long distance to the city.
I shall go back that long distance to the city.

This is the most loved of all of Saisei's fine little lyrics. The six poems gathered under the title of "A Strange Landscape" were all written in his hometown of Kanazawa. Of the six, this one is the most impressive.

There is, however, a general misunderstanding regarding the poem; namely, that the poem comes out of Saisei's wretched life in the city. This misunderstanding was even advanced by Hagiwara Sakutarō who was very familiar with Saisei's life and poetry. The source of the misunderstanding is found in the poem proper. The first line might suggest that the poet is in Tokyo, singing a nostalgic song. Because Kanazawa was called Kanazawa City, Sakutarō chose to believe that Saisei was in Tokyo singing about Kanazawa, whereas, to the contrary, he was in Kanazawa, referring in the refrain to Tokyo.

It is more understandable that we should take the poem as an outburst of indignation on the part of a man who was rejected in his hometown. This aptly explains ll.1-5. Back in Tokyo, however, some nostalgia for his hometown will be felt, especially when evening falls. Even now, on the verge of leaving Kanazawa, he well knows that some homesickness will ensue when he is gone. He clearly anticipates his inevitable homesickness. If one asks what the poem is about, it is the love-hate feelings the poet has regarding his hometown.

ISHIKAWA TAKUBOKU

"Smoke"—4 tanka
(from *A Handful of Sand*)

Today
nostalgia burns in my heart
like a high fever.
Smoke in the blue sky
is exquisitely poignant.

I say my name softly
and tears fill my eyes.
The fourteen years
of my springtime
are irretrievably lost.

Okane's ringing words
resound in Sojiro's ears.
At dusk,
the stark whiteness
of radish flowers....

I gaze at
my hometown mountains
and am speechless.
Hometown mountains,
I simply say—thank you.

Section 2—"Smoke"—contains tanka of longing for his hometown. He spent his junior high-school years in Morioka and the reminiscences of those days are found in the first part of "Smoke". The second part of "Smoke" contains memories of people and nature in Shibutami Village, his hometown. Battered by life in Tokyo, longing for the joy of his boyhood days, he must have felt, was as futile as trying to follow "Smoke in the blue sky". Most of these tanka were written in 1910 when he could not help but feel the intractability of the times. He had been gravely shocked by the anarchist's High Treason Incident of 1910.

But at the same time he continually fanned the fires of nostalgia for his hometown.

In another tanka he speaks of leaving his hometown as a man being "hounded out by villagers with their stones." His father, Kazusada, was head priest of Hōtokuji Temple of the Sōtō Zen sect, but in 1904 was dismissed by the Religious Affairs Office of that sect. Although the punishment was rescinded in 1906, his desire to be reinstated as head priest was not granted. Moreover the temple communications were split into two hopelessly divided camps and as a result, finding the agony insupportable, Kazusada fled, in March 1907. His family hopes thus destroyed, they all dispersed in disarray and Takuboku's nomadic life in Hokkaido began.

Takuboku never saw his hometown again. His love for nature in Shibutami Village conflicted with his hatred of those who had ousted his family. We find nature in his tanka celebrated in such references as "the mountains and rivers/of my boyhood" and the banks of the Kitakami River that "rise before me." He was permanently wedded to the natural wonders of his hometown. His "boyhood" mountains are Mt. Iwate and Mt. Himekami, visible from Shibutami Village. Taken with a sudden yearning to hear "his hometown dialect," he suddenly went to Ueno Train Station where he could hear it. This brought back innumerable memories of his fellow-villagers. A hack driver—the Sōjiro of the tanka—as soon as he had money, immediately squandered it on drink. His wife Okane (signifying both money and bell) was always bawling and squalling in protest. Takuboku evokes the villagers' poverty and hardship in his heartfelt tanka.

As a junior high-school student, Takuboku sometimes crawled out his classroom window and escaped to sprawl on the grass of Morioka Castle (also called Kozukata Castle). As an example of affection for his hometown:

A Handful of Earth
(from *Now I Can Hear*)

'Just for one day, god,
please don't disturb the people's sleep
in my hometown.'
Thus I've always prayed.
Thinking each day my last,
I've always been overcome with grief,
but the god has never granted my wish.
Just for one day
to return to my hometown unobserved,

weeping to my heart's content!
I'd hold a handful of earth where my home used to be,
and quickly sneak away.
I hope for nothing but that my wish be granted.

In this poem Takuboku's extreme sense of having been ostracized by his fellow
townsmen is keenly felt. The trip from Hokkaido he made by ship rather than
train in order to avoid meeting any fellow-townsmen. He wishes in poetry that
for one day the god would not waken the villagers so that he could sneak into
his town and grasp one handful of dirt on the spot where his house had stood.
We feel a heartrending longing for the Mother Earth that had given him birth
and succor.

YAMAMURA BOCHŌ

Hometown
(from *A Treetop Nest*)

Ah, I can see a quiet, beautiful lake
through the four or five dead trees.
The trees and mountains that ring the lake are dark even by day.
They seem artificial.
How terribly lonely, this place!
An uncertain lonesome narrow path seems to disappear
on a hillside.
But the chimney
of a forbidding hut
exhales a streak of white smoke
like a thread.
Memory is so acute!
Like a baby's eye this clear lake
nestles in the bosom of the mountain.
In the dead of winter
at ice-cutting time
my father worked there
like a bear among men.
He remains iron-hard, as ever.
Hey, brother, how's that old woman
who tends the tea-hut on the pass?

The cuckoo she caught in the vale
she cherished and took pride in
as if it were her child or grandchild.
That old woman—
is she still alive?

Bochō (born Kogure Hakujū) was the son of a farmer in Munataka,
Tsutsumi-ga-oka Village, Gumma Prefecture. Raised in trying familial
circumstances, the child had to move from place to place. His father's efforts at
cutting ice blocks on Lake Haruna at the foot of the mountain of the same name
are alluded to. The ice was cut in a place where people now skate and where
smelt are taken in ice fishing. The road the bus follows now is not the old road.
The back road leads from Munakata up across the Nanamagari Road, crosses
Jizō Pass, heads down past Haruna Shrine and so to the lakeside. This once was
probably the main road.

The entire poem is based on boyhood memories: the desolate ice-cutting
milieu where his father labored with other tough men; in that lonely, forlorn
setting the lake as clear as "a baby's eye"; the retrospective glance at the trees
and mountains ringing the lake as black as "artificial" products. The old woman
at the tea-hut who truly treasured her cuckoo warmly lights this landscape. The
poem ends on a note of nostalgia as Bochō enquires of his brother, "is she still
alive?"

HAGIWARA SAKUTARŌ

The New Koide Road
(from *Pure Lyriacal Pieces*)

This new road leads
straight to the city.
Standing at these crossroads, I am unable
to see a real horizon.
Ah, what a dismal day.
The sky lowers to the eaves of the houses.
Various trees have been felled here and there.
No, damn it! Give me my memories back!
All the young trees have been cut down—
I'll never travel this road again.

The road from Maebashi (his hometown) to Koidegawara (now Shikishima Park) by the Tone River, Sakutarō himself arbitrarily named The New Koide Road. The locale had before been a lane under a canopy of leaves that he was fond of walking, so that a fine old country road was now a paved road to the city; in the process the copse was cleared and a row of houses was built; thus indignation and sorrow together aroused him. "No, damn it! Give me my memories back!" But the past is past. Standing alone at the crossroads on this gloomy day, he no longer desires to walk. It would be unbearable. He refuses to proceed along this new road. The felled trees are now a myriad raw stumps lining the road.

The destruction of nature in his hometown is equivalent to the rude amputation of his limbs.

Kunisada Chūji's Grave Marker
(from *Ice Island*)

Sericulture had already ceased in the Joshū District
when I came back to this village.
The farm houses all show winter shutters.
The sun is dark in the dusty air.
A bamboo grove throws a ghastly shadow.
I feel the very misery of human deprivation.
Look! Here stands a useless stone.
This sleeping outlaw's stone stands
in the midst of wind-blown bamboo grasses.

Ah, me....I wander around my hometown
and come to this loneliest of all spots.
Though he had abandoned his family long ago
and lived from minute-to-minute
the life of a gambler, fate destroyed him
and here he lies in this desolate field.
Even though I try to renew my own life,
you here under this desolate winter stone
convince me that life is a dead end.

—at Kunisada Village in the Jōshū District—

"A brief note on my poem" by Sakutarō reads as follows:

> In the winter of 1930 I had returned to my hometown
> to care for my ill father. At that time I was completely
> discouraged by everything I was trying to do, so I
> could hardly bear the severe, gnawing hunger of my
> heart. I sneaked quietly out of the house and rode a
> bicycle to Kunisada Village on a gusty, dusty day.
> Chūji's grave marker lay by the roadside in that cold,
> desolate place. It seemed nothing more than a tiny
> molehill shuddering in the dark shadows of a bamboo
> thicket. The winter sun being so dark, I couldn't help
> but think of the dismal life of an outlaw. Not until I
> took a look around did I begin to realize that nature in
> this Jōshū District is fiercer and crueler than I had yet
> thought.

Beneath Chūji's marker—"A useless stone"—lay a man the world could do
without—a son of Belial. But for Sakutarō back there in his hometown after
himself having suffered reduced circumstances, and being idle to boot, Chūji
did not seem a total stranger. His own personal fate was one he apparently had
to endure: that of "an outlaw's sleep" in the shivering shadow of a dark bamboo
thicket in a cold, desolate village. The presence of a "useless stone" on a
desolate wintry field tore at his heart.

YAGI JŪKICHI (1898-1927)

A Plain Koto
(from *A Poor Christian*)

Place a plain koto in this brightness
and low notes will begin
spontaneously reverberating
in its impatience for autumn's beauty.

A Child

A hill and a field
where slight trees
stood sparse

and trembling....
an early spring afternoon
in its roundness;
a wretched child
stared at me,
rolling his eyes.

Hometown

Even today as I sink into the abysm of my heart
my hometown sparkles as on a festive occasion.

Jūkichi died a devout Christian at age twenty-nine in 1927. "A Plain Koto" is inscribed on a monument by his old home in Aihara Oto in Sakai Village (now Machida City) in the Minami-tama District.

The beauty and brightness of autumn as comparable to a poet's heart begins to be heard sympathetically in this poem. It is a good example of Jūkichi's naively natural and beautiful, if simple, poetry.

His heart never strays from the beautiful idyllic landscape of his hometown encircled by the Tama Hills. It is both beautiful and recalled simply. His poems lack altogether the discordant hometown feelings that are present in Takuboku's and Saisei's work. Even in depression he finds his hometown bright and shining "as on a festive occasion."

ITŌ SEI (1905-1969)

Hometown
(from *Winter Night*)

Ahhh! my poor hometown!
The trees are bare,
the mountains shaggy in dusk.
The driving rain soaked
the bottom of my trousers as under my black umbrella
I looked again and again
at the hometown landscape I was leaving.
My father, mother and brothers lived

lonelier than ever in small comfort,
and even that in danger of disappearing.
Ahhh! Is this what I'd come home to!
The station lowered its head in the rain,
trains stood silently side by side, their lights glaring,
their hollow cheeks sunken in shadows.
Ahhh, that I had to leave my town in this condition!
It seemed the winter snows would kill and bury it.

Sei's hometown was in the suburbs of Otaru in Hokkaido. He tells us his feelings as he waited in the winter rain in a hometown he had long been absent from.

"Ahhh! my poor hometown!"—the first line—is pregnant with his true feelings. His family members were living in straightened circumstances. The bare trees present a hometown that is forlorn and helpless, and he unexpectedly wonders if this is what he has returned for. Under the surface he feels a prick of conscience for abandoning town and family and returning alone to the city.

A couple of years ago I visited Otaru for the first time and found it a charming place no longer prospering. When I met Mr. Itō back in Tokyo I told him what a nice place I thought it was. He smiled and said, "Yes, everyone says that—now that it's in decline." Travellers find the place to be quiet and pleasant whereas the poet feels his heart eaten away by the demise of his hometown.

TANAKA FUYUJI

In My Hometown
(from *A Walk Under the Pale Moon*)

Ah, the smell of dried dab being grilled.
It's near lunchtime in my lonely hometown.

The house roofs of those
whose livelihood is drying dab
are weighted with stones.

It's near lunchtime in my lonely hometown.
On the deserted white street
a mountain snow-monger walks alone.
—A teenage memory of the Ecchū District—

Fuyuji's hometown is in Toyama Prefecture, though he was born in Fukushima City. After his father's death he was placed in the care of his relatives in Tokyo. In 1910, when he was sixteen he visited his father's home during the summer vacation in Oiji-cho in Toyama Prefecture. At this time he spent some weeks with his younger brother who had been cared for by his grandmother. This poem presumably recalls that summer.

The village was the small one his father abandoned in the mountains and Fuyuji was visiting. This dismal landscape seems appropriate to the town's lonely fate. "A mountain snow-monger" is a man who in winter quarries and piles up snow in an ice-house and sells it in the villages in summer.

MURANO SHIRŌ

A Mournful Hometown Melody
(from *A Club of Coral*)

The fishes of my childhood are no longer
found in the brook. The brook bed reveals to my sight
only porcelain shards and cans. Where have they all gone,
those fish with their beautiful rainbow ventrals,
fanning the water with their tails?
They must have died out. They still
swim in my memory, bright as water weeds,
and I can't count how often I have dreamed in my city life
of chasing after those fish. When I look now
all I see is one thin newt poking along
through the roots of the water weeds.
Everything I hate most has outlived everything I love.

A frog croaking in a treetop
takes shelter in the farthest corner
of the Tama District.

Shirō was born in the western suburbs of Tokyo in the Tama District, now called Fuchū City. The male chub in springtime sports a crimson bar along its belly, in the mating season. This is the beautiful fish he refers to in the brook of his hometown which now overflows in his memory in nostalgic recollection of his youth. Now they are gone from the brook; in their place is a scattering of porcelain shards and tin cans. A single newt walks on the bed of the brook.

Although the poem treats a couple of tiny creatures, Shiro is heart-stricken over the vast changes that have relentlessly occurred to the boyhood landscape he so fondly remembers. The Musashino Plains remain permanently in a corner of the poet's mind and heart.

MARUYAMA KAORU

Love without Words
(from *Inside a Flower*)

When I walk in deep snow
around the mountain top
or under the trees at sunset,
I am suddenly reminded
of my deceased mother
or my dear wife at home.

I recall the small kindnesses of women
I met in passing—
who were just as suddenly gone.

Nature has absorbed them all.
Their passing, at times like the wind,
plays upon my heart strings—love without words.

Because of his father's having been an official in the Ministry of Home Affairs Kaoru moved from place to place during his childhood. So the idea of a hometown meant for him virtually nothing: "My enforced removal from place to place willy-nilly fostered in me a sort of outsider's perspective."

In May 1945, he fled to Iwanezawa in Nishiyamamura, Yamagata Prefecture, hoping to escape the dangers of the war. There he spent three years as a local grade school teacher. His mother Take died soon after the war ended. The "deceased mother" of l. 5 tells us that the poem was written during those years when he lived in the north country mountain village.

Enduring the severe, lonely winters of the north country, he recalled rather kaleidoscopically the woman he had known—his mother, his present wife and others who had disappeared soon after chance encounters. And he claims that the memories of all these women dissolved into loneliness itself in nature, playing a melody of "love without words." He is filled with warm gratitude for their many "small kindnesses".

ONO TŌZABURŌ (1903-1996)

Tomorrow
(from *Osaka*)

Old reeds have withered.
Buds are few and far between.
A flock of snipes pass like a cloud over the river.
A violent wind tears at the sandbar.
The spring tide is turbid.
Above the cracking of the reeds I hear
the wind blowing through the industrial district.
Something seems awry.
I can't fathom what.
My lenses reveal sporadic desolation.
In the absence of light and sound
a deep shade
invades the horizon.
Iron, nickel,
India rubber, sulfuric acid, nitrogen, magnesium—
these alone.

Tōzaburō was born in Naniwa-shinchi, Osaka City, which was built on a triangular sandbank between tributary streams of the Yodo River. It was originally an extensive reedy marsh and so the poet Saigyō in writing the following waka had referred to Naniwa as a "reed-scattering" place (it serves as a "pillow word", or a kind of conventional epithet):

The beautiful spring landscape
of Naniwa in Tsu-no-kuni—
was it but a dream?
Through the endless expanse of withered reeds
the wind whispers, whispers.

The marsh land had been reclaimed. Even the vestiges of what Tōzaburō calls the "reedy province" are gone. Beyond the reeds he hears the wind passing through the factory area. The landscape he described in "Tomorrow" is today a reality. The devastation found in his hometown took place in a mere wink of time, as of a person dozing off and immediately awaking.

KUSANO SHIMPEI

Kami-Ogawa Village
(from *Peony Garden*)

By day the purple of milk vetch and wisteria.
By night the *Whoo-hoo* of the owl.

Next to each other: A tin smith, clog shop, peasant,
tatami maker, blacksmith, Oshin-chan,
a lively stable and the horseshoer Hiko.
None of these shops existed in the distant past.
The villagers numbered sixteen or seventeen.
The vein of a brook ran through the village,
        teeming with trout and catfish.
A deer secured to a log was carried along.
In those days Shirai Empei was born and reared here,
as was Kushida Tamizō.
A few such unusual fellows remain even now.
Good-natured old Kusano Sennosuke is still alive,
bald as a cue ball, looking like a sea goblin.

By day the purple of milk vetch and wisteria.
By night the *Whoo-hoo* of the owl.

Kami-Ogawa Village, Fukushima Prefecture—Shimpei's hometown—is now Iwaki City. The summary layout and life of the village humorously concludes with the memory of Oshin-chan's house.

Shirai Empei was a Diet member, Kushida Tamizō was a Marxist economist and Kusano Sennosuke was Shimpei's relative. The latter is an example of the unusual men produced by this very small village, Shimpei himself being the outstanding figure. A mere list of names of course falls flat on general readers; likewise, Takuboku and Kōtarō, however, make similar lists in their poems. Yet even readers unacquainted with such names may develop amicable sentiments about them.

ITŌ SHIZUO

Homecomers
(from *Summer Flowers*)

Nature is unspeakably beautiful
and people are eternally poverty-stricken.
I have seen the froth of waves
grumble to themselves
in returning to the shore
as they repeatedly assault the rocks.
Hometowners come back again
are always just the same as that,
though their soliloquies smack
more of common sense than compassion.
('Gee, nothing beautiful here now!')
Why 'now'?
From the very beginning,
'beautiful hometown' are words that have been
homework impossible for people to complete.
I cannot believe that people
have ever lived as beautifully
as nature lives.
After endless trials and tribulations
homecomers have always ended in the grave
to find at least
a measure of comfort and joy.

Envoi

I who have deserted my hometown......
O city, how dare I call myself at home in you!

I who have learned to write poems......
How dare I not long for a life of deeds!

The poem was written in 1934. The first two lines convey a sense of both severity and beauty. The desolation of waves splattering upon the rocks is not the landscape of Shizuo's hometown, Isahaya. The image is, however, indispensable in expressing feelings about his hometown, Isahaya. The parenthetical line, "Gee, nothing beautiful here now" as spoken by homecomers has never been true. His claim "beautiful hometown" is a patent falsehood; people thrive on complaints and pain, and are afterwards altered into monuments, all of which gives Shizuo solace.

In his life in Osaka alone does the sense of an invariably beautiful hometown live in his heart. Behind the poem lie the bitterness and pain he experienced as the result of his father Sōkichi's death in 1932 when he inherited an estate in arrears and was forced to abandon both it and his hometown.

Extreme sadness must follow for such a man living in Osaka whose lost hometown must now seem cruelly beautiful. He who has such an aching heart is alone entitled to speak of "homework" that is in vain.

Waking from a Dream
(from *Summer Flowers*)

What has startled me from my dream at this hour?
Out the window on far-off Mimihara Goryo Hillside
a fire....which makes my heart pound,
I don't know why. I don't know why?
Ah, I have been dreaming of my hometown house!
The doors of the big house open, I sat alone on tatami
looking at the trees and flowers, and sipping sake.
The evening sun slipped under the eaves,
its light too beautiful for eyes to fathom,
a light cool and clear and without expression.
White flowers shining on the trees in the glow of evening sat
upright
and I recalled myself, a child unable to cling to her sleeve.
Oh! What wakened me was—yes!—not the eerie cry of the night
bird at Mimihara Goryo.
It was the sadness of the song I sang as I dreamed.

There under the azure sky
my mother sits;
sits atop a dead tree

that glitters above the snowy ravine
in spring.
Ah, I see her
sitting atop that tree.

The poem treats a former home of Itō Shizuo in his hometown, Isahaya, as seen in a dream. He was now living near the imperial mausoleum of Emperor Nintoku called Mozu-no-Mimihara-Nakano-Misasagi. Hatsu, his mother, had died some two years earlier.

Drinking, looking out upon white blossoms on a tree in the garden (probably a cucumber tree), he is moved to recall his mother's erect posture (the blossoms seem also sitting erect) and is unable to grasp the sleeve of her kimono. The whole is a dream vision.

The vision takes place "under the azure sky...above a snowy ravine," that is, an immaculate place out of mere human reach. That he can never again see his mother is compressed in the voice that sings in a literary style, as compared with the colloquialism of the preceding stanza.

IKADAI KAICHI (1899-1971)

Homecoming
(from *Miscellaneous Tanka at My Bamboo Hut, Riu*)

Departure

While I would not intend
for it to be my farewell journey
in this world,
I long passionately
to see my hometown once again.

I try to enumerate
the hometown dead
but my memory is buried.
I contemplate my journey
but I cannot count them all.

I am troubled by
gifts I ought to take.
Is this because somehow
some of them
still weigh on my mind?

I rush almost headlong
to return there,
though fewer
and fewer people
wait for me to grow gray hair.

The Beach at Amabarashi

At the inn in my hometown,
Amabarashi,
I spent one night,
thinking of the waves
I heard as a boy.

The Port

My first love
has long since married
and grown old.
Could I see her now
my bitter sweet memories would vanish.

Takaoka City

My hometown has become for me
a foreign land.
Look as I will,
I find nothing familiar
but the road.

My parents' house
is but a stone's throw away
but I choose
to avoid it.
Let it live in my memory.

My hometown is cresting
on a wave of 'modernization,'
as though it deliberately
flaunted
my dogged attachment to it.

Kojo Park

I stand alone
before my father's monument.
Father, I have already
outlived you
by ten years.

The grassy field I played in
is long gone.
But even this half-century later,
I stumble about
in search of that field.

Saiji Temple at Kosugi-chō

I stoop and pick
blades of grass I had long forgotten.
Now I bow and close my eyes
and place prayerful palm to palm
before my parents' monument.

Kaichi hailed from Toyama Prefecture's Takaoka City. Takenomon, his father, was renowned as a haiku poet in the Meiji period. In the early 1960s the city was already involved in the throes of "modernization" as a prefectural industrial center. At that point a gray-haired old tanka poet returned for what he hoped would not be the last time.

The familiar road he trod is lined on both sides with unfamiliar houses and so he is helpless to search for acquaintances. The field where he played is gone. Because it would break his heart, he opts not to take a look at the house he once lived in, now utterly altered. To run into his former love would only destroy his sweet memories, so he decides not to see her. The waves that break on Amabarashi Beach are unchanged, unchanging. The beach is famous in folklore as a spot where Minamoto-no-Yoshitsune stopped to pray for clear skies.

Hometowns have a way of becoming strange to us. As a rule, our flesh itself "remembers a hometown"; it is a place where in some odd corner or by a brook we rediscover, recall ourselves. Even though a cord of the heart has been cut away, we still speak of "hometown," and do so even while knowing that the quest is in vain.

INDEX